Despite its rich Christian heritage, it is deeply troubling that today's Europe is fast becoming a neglected mission field with a declining Christian presence. But despite the challenges, you can't miss the urgent enthusiasm of the authors that today is a moment of unique opportunity for the gospel. In this timely book, they describe both the complexities and the priorities of European mission, and demonstrate that engagement in this task is not only essential but truly possible for every believer. A great resource for every church!

Jonathan Lamb

Formerly, IFES Regional Secretary for Europe and Eurasia,
and Director of Langham Preaching

At a time when Europe's political and social future is on many people's minds, yet the understanding of Europe's spiritual condition tends to lag behind, such an informed, balanced, and well thought-through reflection as is found in this book, is a breath of fresh air. It provides detailed research, is well organized and equally well argued by two highly competent British authors, who bring a depth of understanding, combined with an unrivalled experience of the current European realities. They do not shy away from the complex and the difficult, yet show the good and the possible, as they argue for the importance of reaching Europe with the gospel, when many have given up on this part of the world.

The reader will find here an exceptionally helpful, desperately needed introduction to the intricacies of the history of Europe and how it influences the current spiritual climate of wider Europe. This analysis is followed by suggestions for possible strategic ways forward if Europe is to be reached for Christ, with a direct challenge to consider again mission in Europe.

As a Christian, and a European who is passionate about the expansion of the Kingdom of God in Europe, I warmly recommend that you take time to dive into this fascinating book. However, I warn you that, besides being enlightened by it, the book will also challenge you!

Dr. Andrzej Turkanik

Executive Director, Quo Vadis Institute, Salzburg, Austria

Two excellent thinkers share their common pa
book is *readable*—even if in contrasting styles;
and *challenging*—thanks to their vision and va

GH00771887

considering the present complicated situation of Europe which desperately needs mission. Read the book, and you'll understand why!

Fāres Marzone
Bible teacher and writer, and formerly Principal of the
Italian Evangelical Bible Institute, Rome

McQuoid and Summerton set out to write a book that would help the reader to understand Europe in all its complexity and spiritual need. In nine short chapters, they review the history of Christianity in Europe, the contemporary spiritual context, and the practice of Christian mission that is appropriate today. As the authors themselves put it, "this is a serious book for those who take Europe seriously". I heartily recommend it and pray it gets widely read.

Jim Memory
Co-Regional Director for Europe, Lausanne Movement
MA Tutor for Mission in Europe, All Nations Christian College

Europe needs Jesus. That might be one way of summing up this book. The authors' aim is to inform the reader about the state of faith in Europe, from Greenland to the Russian frontier, and to encourage us to be the answer through engagement in mission. And they succeed in this aim.

It is tempting, and a temptation some evangelicals in the UK fall into, to decry the state of Europe (by which they usually mean continental Europe) and speak of the decline in Christianity with an almost masochistic schadenfreude. McQuoid and Summerton do not fall into this trap. They do not shy away from the realities of the situation in Europe, but, through their use of real-life missionary experience and clear call to mission engagement, they show that the Europe of today is still a place where the good news of Jesus can be proclaimed and new life can flourish.

The various statistics used are helpful for understanding the context—though they are, by their nature, out of date even before they are printed. The appendices, especially Appendix F which summarizes the key political institutions in Europe, are very helpful. I am involved daily with mission in Europe in a different organisation from GLO, and the contribution that the book makes to mission in Europe is welcome and to be supported.

Simon Marshall
International Director, European Christian Mission International

EUROPE
AT THE
SPIRITUAL
CROSSROADS

STEPHEN MCQUOID
AND NEIL SUMMERTON

2024

Contents

List of Illustrations and Maps

Introduction

Books are written for a purpose. Some tell a good story, to absorb and entertain their readers. Others are books that educate: they give information that the reader can learn from and therefore be more knowledgeable. Still others are written to challenge and to make the reader think.

This book has also been written with a clear purpose in mind. That is to help the reader understand just how complicated and spiritually needy Europe is and to challenge readers to make Europe a prayer and mission priority. It is also a book that is passionate about the gospel because both authors have a conviction that the gospel, which is the good news of Jesus Christ, is ultimately the only real hope that our world has.

Over the past 50 years, GLO has been involved in bringing the gospel to Europe using short-term mission teams as well as long-term missionaries. For all of us, 2024 is a very significant year because it is GLO's anniversary. For half a century we have prayed and evangelised our way across Europe. We have planted churches in the process and developed a range of different ministry opportunities.

GLO, of course, is only one of many organisations and churches involved in the evangelisation of Europe. God has blessed and many people have become Christians—and for that we give God thanks. Despite all of this, Europe today is as needy as ever. Need is a relative thing, as there are spiritual needs everywhere. However, the facts speak for themselves. Europe has the lowest proportion of evangelical Christians of any continent in the world. Indeed, African evangelicals outnumber their European counterparts by a factor of 10 to 1. This means that you are more likely to meet a Christian on the streets of Delhi, Cairo, or even Doha, than you would be in Belgrade, Athens, or Ljubljana. This stark reality reminds us that Europe must continue to be a mission destination. We need to do all we can to reach this needy continent and bring the good news of the gospel to it.

This, of course, is easier said than done. The wealth and comfort that most Europeans enjoy has often served to distract them from their spiritual needs. Moreover, Europe has become progressively more secularist and increasingly suspicious of Christian belief. In general, Europeans are resistant when it comes to the proclamation of the gospel, and therefore evangelism in Europe is not for the faint-hearted. The staggering church growth that we see taking place across the world, and especially in sub-Saharan Africa, China and Latin America, has simply not been replicated in Europe. God is at work throughout Europe, but it is a hard place when it comes to spreading the gospel.

Our prayer as you read this book is that you will realise what a huge challenge it is to evangelise Europe, but also how important it is that we do so. We hope you will find this book interesting and that you will learn what a complex and fascinating place Europe is. It is intended to be a serious book for people who take Europe seriously and want to understand it so that they can witness. Most Christians in the UK, and indeed in Europe as a whole, don't really know much of the history, politics, culture and challenge of this significant part of the world. This book aims to fill in the blanks and enable you to begin to grasp the context in which we live and need to witness. More importantly, we hope that you will be challenged to pray for Europe and to be open to being used by God to reach Europeans for Christ and to support God's work there.

This book is the product of two authors with different, but complementary, styles of writing. Chapters 1, 4, 5, 7, 8, 9, 10 and appendices A–D were written by Stephen and chapters 2, 3, and 6 and appendices E and F by Neil. Some chapters have a tendency to make use of the first person singular and also contain personal illustrations, while others do not. These differences in style are common in dual-authored works. Also many of the chapters finish with a connecting statement which is in bold type. The purpose of these is to link chapters and also demonstrate the progression and systematic logic of the book. Our hope is that clarity will not be sacrificed, and that readers will observe the gospel passion that motivates both authors.

Chapter 1

How did we get to here?

Many of us have had the experience of walking along a beach and discovering sets of footprints in the sand. Some of these footprints may be deep and easy to see, others more shallow and less obvious. However, each one is evidence that someone has been here before. When we think about modern-day Europe, one thing that becomes immediately apparent is that Europe is a very diverse place, composed of lots of different peoples. It is a relatively small continent compared with the others, but it has many more separate nation states than others—approaching fifty in fact. And even within quite small nation states, there can be differing cultures. When we look a little closer, we realise that there are also different worldviews and belief systems. While pretty well all will be recognizably European, there is therefore no such thing as a typical European: different people in Europe will view the world in very different ways.

None of this is accidental, but rather it is a product of history. Europe has evolved over the centuries and the many changes that have taken place throughout history have influenced the lives of people who live there and have left an indelible mark, much like the footprints that we see on a beach. To begin to understand Europe and the people who live here, we need to have a look at European history so that we can see how Europeans today have been shaped and why they believe what they do.

Ancient Europe was a brutal place where pagans worshipped gods such as Thor and Odin, or the deities of the Greek and Roman Empires. This situation changed forever with the advent of Christianity.

Early Christianity in Europe

The early church grew rapidly and spread out from its initial base in Jerusalem. This was despite opposition and then persecution at the hands of both the Jewish religious authorities and the Romans. In time, the gospel spread into Europe with Paul himself ministering in Rome, the very heart of the empire. These early days also saw theological controversies that had to be resolved, not least because the church lacked a hierarchical structure, and the widespread circulation of the completed canon of Scripture was still some time off. Persecution continued, and was often systematic and politically motivated. A change was to come, however, with the advent of the emperor Constantine.

Having succeeded his father, Constantine began to defend his throne against rivals. On the eve of the decisive battle of Milvian Bridge (October 27, 312), he claimed that he saw a flaming cross in the sky with an inscription in Greek reading, 'By this sign conquer'. Whether this was a conversion in biblical terms is debatable, but after winning the battle, he issued an edict of toleration in AD313, restoring to the Church any confiscated property and making restitution for other losses.

The Emperor Constantine, legalised
Christianity in the Roman Empire

Constantine's support of Christianity not only gave it a stronger foothold in Europe; it also made Rome the centre of gravity of Christian activity, though, for centuries, Christianity remained much stronger in the former eastern part of the Empire. However, Constantine's buttressing of Christianity was not totally secure until the end of the fourth century—there was a reversion to paganism under Emperor Julian in the 360s.

It was only gradually that Christianity spread northwards into Europe and eastwards into the area beyond the Rhine and Danube rivers. This was evidenced by the fact that Rome's mission to England began only in AD597, while at broadly the same time Patrick and others were extending Christianity in Ireland and Scotland. It was a couple of centuries later that Boniface (of Devon in the English kingdom of Wessex) began his mission in Teutonic lands, which included modern Germany. It was the Middle Ages before Crusades sought to extend Christian control into the north-eastern marches of Europe, such as the area of the modern Baltic states, and Orthodox Christianity was established in what is now Ukraine.

Meanwhile, as the church became more hierarchical, the simplicity of the New Testament church life began to disappear. Leo the Great (390–461) was the first church leader to be given the title of 'Pope' and the position of Bishop of Rome became entrenched as primary in the Church. When the Roman Empire finally crumbled, the church continued and developed into the Middle Ages.

The Middle Ages

By the early Middle Ages, Christianity was well established throughout the Mediterranean and south-western Europe, though at the same time it came under threat from the advance of Islam in Spain and even France, and from the pagan Vikings from the north. (However, Viking settlements in places such as Normandy and Sicily soon converted to Christianity.) With the collapse of the western Roman Empire after AD400 and the fragmentation of rule that resulted, the church often held society together locally. The western Catholic church became a unifying force wherever it existed and gained significant in-fluence in civic as well as spiritual affairs. In time, great cathedrals, monasteries, and eventually universities were demonstrations of the church's influence and power, and the Pope was not just a religious leader: he was arguably Europe's most powerful political leader as well. By the late Middle Ages, Europe still had its Jews and Muslims, but they tended to be persecuted minorities. No one from within or outside of Europe could threaten the dominance of Christian beliefs and there was no credible alternative, though the Church did have its reform movements from within (the Franciscan and Dominican friars) and seceders, whether biblically orthodox like the followers of Wycliffe in England and Hus in Bohemia or heretics, like the Cathars in southern France.

The influence of the church could be seen in the legal system and through education. Whereas Europe's greatest minds had previously devoted themselves to philosophy, they were now devoting themselves to theology, because it was believed that all knowledge was ultimately revealed by God.

As David Wells comments, the medieval thinkers 'were convinced that God's revelation, of which they were custodians, was true. True in an absolute sense. It was not merely true to them; it was not merely true in their time; it was not true approximately. What God had given was true universally, absolutely, enduringly'.[1] This attitude to truth made the Church the interpreter of truth and, therefore, more often than not, the builder of the universities. The Church, that is the Roman Church, dominated the intellectual life of Europe, and therefore rulers sought to control it, leading to schisms and competing popes in the later Middle Ages.

It should be remembered that for most Europeans at this time, Europe was the centre of their world (though they were aware that the Crusades were campaigning in another part of the world, and that they also needed to venture into the wider world to trade for essential commodities). Their Europe was expanding as the Scandinavian north was brought into the fold of the Roman church, the Castilians reconquered the Iberian Peninsula from the Muslim Moors, and small extensions were made on the north-eastern Marches. However, the Europe that they thought about was still only a part of what we now regard as Europe.

---

1. David Wells, *No Place for Truth* (Grand Rapids MI: Eerdmans 1993), pp. 259–60.

The Renaissance

This situation was not to last because a huge cultural change known as the Renaissance swept throughout Europe. This was a time of reawakening with explorers such as Marco Polo discovering new worlds and writing perhaps the most influential travel book of all time.

Artists such as Michelangelo were reawakening the classical art of sculpture and painting, and increasingly non-Christian themes were being depicted as classical myths were celebrated. The field of writing was also developing, and these new thinkers began to suggest that learning was an end in itself and not just something that should be done and controlled by the Church. The Dutch scholar, Erasmus, devoted himself to the study of particularly New Testament Greek, and the renaissance scholars studied ancient writings that were not specifically Christian.

The Renaissance was to impact Europe deeply and this in turn was partly to give birth to the Reformation which split Europe and led to 200 years of religious wars in western and central Europe. Both the Renaissance and the Reformation created conditions for modern science and engineering to emerge because of their promotion of independent thought. This was also helped by the opening of Europe to a wider world.

One of the key thinkers of the Renaissance was Francis Bacon (1561–1626) who has often been described as the first modern scientist.[2] He was a contemporary of the Italian astronomer, Galileo Galilei (1564–1642) who caused a controversy by arguing that the earth was not the centre of the planetary system, but the sun. Bacon used experimentation as a way of finding new discoveries and he believed that science could lead to a better society. He was not alone: there was his contemporary, the German astronomer, Johannes Kepler (1571–1630), and, in the mid-seventeeth century, natural scientists in Britain.

---

2. Stanley J. Grenz, *A Primer on Postmodernism* (Grand Rapids MI: Eerdmans, 1996), p. 58.

Francis Bacon, a founder of modern scientific method

Galileo, whose revised explanation of the solar
system led to the charge of heresy and house
arrest in Rome in the last years of his life.

Isaac Newton was only one of a group of thinkers
in England and Scotland who contributed to
remarkable advances in scientific understanding
(with roots deep in the religious life of the time).

The Reformation

Hot on the heels of the Renaissance came the Reformation which also helped
to pave the way for intellectual and political developments which shaped
Europe. The Reformation made several significant contributions to European
life. First, it established the principle that individuals could interpret Scripture
for themselves, rather than deferring to the Church's interpretation. Secondly, it
encouraged independence of thought and individualism which helped prepare
the way for the eventual advent of democracy.

The Counter-Reformation served only to continue this process—indeed
Ignatius of Loyola, founder of the Jesuits who were at the forefront of the
Counter-Reformation, essentially accepted many of the underlying assumpt-
ions of the Reformation. What is interesting is that most of the Reformers
were happy to accept the same kind of relationship between church and state
as did the Catholic church, which resulted in many of the Protestant European

countries having a state church, just as Catholic countries saw Catholicism as their state church. Only the Anabaptists tended to propose the separation of church and state.

The Enlightenment

The significance of the Renaissance lay not so much in its own achievements, but also in opening the door for the Enlightenment in the seventeenth and eighteenth centuries. The first and one of the most influential Enlightenment thinkers was the mathematician, René Descartes (1596–1650). If Bacon was the founder of modern science, Descartes was the founder of modern philosophy.[3] Born in La Haye in France, Descartes studied law at La Flèche and Poitiers, before travelling extensively in Europe. At Ulm in Germany, Descartes began to write on the subject of philosophy and completed his first major work in the 1620s. He believed in God and was concerned that some thinkers were rejecting the medieval worldview of knowledge through revelation and were becoming sceptical about the very existence of God. Descartes decided to devise a method of discovering truth that could be reliable. His ultimate aim was to devise a rational apologetic for God, but that is not how the process turned out.

Descartes' approach is summed up in the Latin phrase, *Cogito ergo sum*, which means, 'I think, therefore I am'. His method was to begin by doubting everything, even his own existence! Next, he thought about the rationality of that position. He concluded that, as he was thinking, he must exist, for only something that exists can have thoughts. He would then note that his existence was objectively true, but a truth that he had verified, not one that had simply been revealed by God. This, he believed, proved that truth could be discovered quite apart from revelation and, further, that human reason was clearly a sure path towards truth.

The impact that Descartes had on subsequent thinking is hard to overstate. Divine revelation began to be replaced by human reason as the fount of knowledge and truth. Someone could now discover the truth about a particular subject without any reference to the Church or to God.

---

3. Diané Collinson, *Fifty Major Philosophers* (London: Routledge, 1997), p. 57.

René Descartes, often regarded as the
first Enlightenment thinker

This new thinking began to influence all branches of knowledge, but especially science. One proponent of this new method, Sir Isaac Newton (1642–1727), believed that the universe was an orderly machine that was predictable in its function and could be understood by discovering the observable laws which governed it. Like Descartes, Newton was a strong theist (with a particular interest in biblical apocalyptic) and he believed that his study of the universe would lead him to wonder at the greatness of God. That, however, was not to be the experience of other scientists. They merely saw this new thinking as a pathway to truth independent of God, and in effect deified human reason.

Medieval thinking did not just disappear, but it ceased to play such an important role during the Enlightenment. Many people still believed in God and were committed to the authority of the Church, so its footprint would remain, and does so even today. Across Europe, Roman Catholics, Orthodox Christians and mainstream Protestants still hold at least some of the worldview of medieval Christianity. But its mark on European life is less pronounced than the one produced by the Reformation and the Enlightenment. The absolute grip that the medieval church once had on the minds of Europeans was broken and has never been repaired.

Enlightenment thinkers continue to make their presence felt, especially in the academy. Some of today's Enlightenment thinkers would label themselves as atheists and others as agnostics. Among the most well-known is Richard Dawkins, one of the leaders of the so-called New Atheists. For them, human reason is supreme, and they have little time for a worldview that acknowledges God. Enlightenment thinking can also be seen in secularism. Many secularists may not be avowedly atheistic; indeed, some believe God exists. But God is just a sideshow or an optional extra. Essentially, they want to live their lives by their own rules and believe that God has no place in the modern world or in public life, except at the level of a hobby.

When we think about the Enlightenment, we need to recognise the good it did, not just for Europe, but the whole of Western society. The belief that people can make new discoveries by applying their powers of reasoning enabled the boundaries of science and engineering to be expanded. We now live in a world of skyscrapers, washing machines, modern medicine, mass transportation and great prosperity. Humankind had progressed and was now mastering the world that they saw around them. All this began with the Enlightenment which projected Western culture to the pinnacle of human civilization. The Christian would say that human beings are able to do this, and make progress, because the universe in which God has set us is ordered and orderly, and humans made in the image of God can by rational inquiry discover how it works.

A crisis for autonomous man

History never stands still, and the positive world of the European Enlightenment was about to be transformed by a series of events which would alter European thinking once more. First, there was the advent of Romanticism, a movement in the late eighteenth century in the arts and literature that emphasized inspiration, subjectivity and the importance of the individual, as a reaction against the mechanistic world of the Age of Reason. This was to shake up the rather rational and predictable Enlightenment thought process. Then came the German philosopher, Friedrich Nietzsche, born in 1844 into a pious Protestant family. He became one of Europe's most creative thinkers.[4] He studied in Bonn and Leipzig before becoming a professor in Basle. As he developed his philosophy, Nietzsche declared that God was dead and that human beings must learn to live life without him.[5]

Friedrich Nietzche, paved the way to postmodernist thought

Nietzsche began to spell out what this should mean in practice. First, if there is no God then there can be no objective way of testing truth. This had not been a problem for medieval thinkers because their truth claims were tested against God's word. Neither was it a problem for people during the Enlightenment because human reason was the sure path to truth. But as Nietzsche rejected both worldviews, the absence of objective truth was clearly a problem. He dealt with this by negating the reality of truth as an absolute and stating that truth was whatever the individual made it. Indeed, it did not matter if a belief was true or not, as long as it was 'life affirming'. In other words, if you believe something, it doesn't matter whether it is actually true, as long as believing it enriches your life.

---

4. Bertrand Russell, *A History of Western Philosophy* (London: Routledge, 1991), p. 728.
5. Friedrich Nietzsche, *The Portable Nietzsche* (New York: Viking, 1968), p. 85.

Secondly, Nietzsche stated that, God being out of the picture, there was no basis for any objective values, meaning or significance in life. Consequently, there was no objective basis for declaring any action to be morally right or wrong. Again, this would not have been the case for medieval or enlightenment thinkers. People in the medieval world had God as their standard for objective ethics and enlightenment thinkers based their ethics on human reason. In both cases, human ethics were objective and firm. For Nietzsche this was not the case. He did feel that morals were important, but there was no way of having an objective moral system because without God there was no means of confirming it.[6]

The net result of Nietzsche's work was that a whole generation of thinkers emerged who thought human life was of little intrinsic value and that objective truth could not be found. Consequently, a change occurred once more in the way in which Europeans dealt with issues of faith and belief. Nietzsche could be described as the father of twentieth-century postmodern relativism, with its crisis of morality, identity and its sexual liberty. In more recent times, this change has also led to the rejection of gender identity based on physical attributes.

The challenge of human progress

This evolution of worldview required more than the writings of one philosopher. Other events were needed. It can be argued that the most important were the two devastating world wars of the twentieth century. It is important to understand the context in which these two great wars occurred. With the development of science and commerce, it was widely believed in the decades preceding World War 1 that humanity was on an upward path of progress. This was an age of optimism and many Europeans thought they were headed towards a kind of Utopia, brought about by the impressive development of science, technology and trade. Moreover, the economic progress and international financial connections that had been established were thought to have

---

6. Linda Smith & William Reaper, *A Beginner's Guide to Ideas: Religion and Philosophy Past and Present* (Oxford: Lion, 1991), p. 168. Nietzsche felt that morals could not just be discovered; rather humans had to create them.

rendered war impossible, as it would be so irrational in such a developed world. It was in this positive atmosphere that World War 1 exploded.

The War was a huge blow to the belief in human progress. Although science had undoubtedly made a positive difference to the lives of many Europeans, it had also produced the mustard gas that was now killing thousands of young men in the trenches. At the end of the war, it was hoped that progress would begin once more; indeed some referred to World War 1 as the 'war to end all wars'. Tragically, however, World War 2 quickly intervened and brought even more carnage. The same science that produced so much good also produced the weapons that destroyed human life on an industrial scale, both on the front line and on the home front. Perhaps most devastating of all psychologically were the nuclear bombs which destroyed Hiroshima and Nagasaki. People were as horrified by this weapon, as they were amazed by its power.

Coupled with this were politically motivated murder, starvation, and genocide on scales that were scarcely credible. Weapons, of course, are in the hands of the people who use them. The political and social organizations produced by the mixture of Enlightenment and Romantic thought were culpable, as death at the hands of the state was occurring on a breath-taking scale, whether by famine, disease or war. Often this was justified by the claim that it was in the interests of a better world. The dream of Utopia based on the certainties of human reason was rapidly coming to an end.

Several more things happened before the Enlightenment dream faded altogether. The advent of big industry and the multinational conglomerates produced many much-needed jobs in the aftermath of the great wars, but they also turned each worker into a statistic on a payroll rather than an individual. People began to lose their sense of worth as they became no more than manufacturing units on the conveyor belt of economic growth. Moreover, big industry, while being the engine of the new world economy, also caused widespread pollution. Clearly this was still progress, but not clean, uncomplicated progress.

Enlightenment thinking had also made an impact on architecture with buildings designed along rational lines to maximize space in an efficient way. Quaint cottages and cobbled streets gave way to huge tower blocks made of concrete and steel. This produced affordable housing for rapidly growing cities, but these new developments were often soulless and soon became crime-ridden ghettoes. Europe was at the cutting edge of world civilization, but at its core there was a deep sickness that was breeding discontent.

Then came the so-called global village. The world was becoming a smaller place as mass transportation became affordable. Europeans began to travel the world to see different cultures, which were found to be apparently working well. Alongside the growing fascination about other parts of the world, there grew within Europe a sense that all was not well. Certainly, Europe had progressed, but the belief in human rationality continued to erode.

This new cultural outlook came to be labelled as postmodernism. This is an overworked term, but one that suggests that the new generation of Europeans had not only rejected medieval thinking, but enlightenment thinking as well, in favour of a more fluid approach. This has produced a kind of split personality in European life. There remains scientific rationalism in some areas, such as depending on science and engineering for the good life that it provides, while at the same time following emotion, instinct and subjective values, sometimes to the point of irrationality, in all other areas of life.

Many Europeans live their lives free of certainty, and questioning traditional approaches to truth and ethics. These Europeans believe in their own truth and relativise morality. They don't reject the idea of God or the spiritual, but do not want their lives to be dictated by such concepts and certainly not by something as outdated and questionable as the Bible. They are also utterly committed to personal freedom and the autonomy of the individual. This is constantly reinforced by both high and popular culture, the world of entertainment and even contemporary psychology. People are encouraged to be themselves and follow their feelings, all of which is very attractive, especially if you want a lifestyle that is free of all restraint.

Postmoderns appreciate what modern technology offers, but technology exists to amplify that freedom and promote the pursuit of leisure and pleasure. They don't want to be forced into any kind of straitjacket. In a previous book, I labelled these as Emergent Europeans and so I will continue to do so in this book.[7]

---

7. See Stephen McQuoid, *Reaching 4 Europes* (Motherwell: GLO Publishing, 2006).

They are now the dominant part of our culture. There are religious Europeans who are influenced by medieval religious thinking. Enlightenment Europeans also exist, many calling themselves atheists or agnostics and clinging to the belief that human rationality can lead to the discovery of objective truth. However, both sets of footprints representing these two worldviews are shallower that those of postmodern Europeans, whose questioning of everything and resistance to conformity is readily apparent.

The new influx

Even now, the story of today's Europe is not finished. Over the last few decades, the population of Europe has been added to by significant numbers of immigrants (though movement of population within and from outside Europe is by no means a new phenomenon). They have descended on Europe from all over the world and from cultures that are utterly different from European culture. Many immigrants into Europe are Christians who have brought a much-needed spiritual vitality. However, many more come from other world religions such as Islam and Hinduism. They have brought the vibrancy of their own cultures with them, but also belief systems that make the evangelisation of Europe an even more uphill task.

This is the Europe of today. Not some monolith, but rather a collection of different people who believe different things and live their lives in different ways. The footprints of all of these groups can be seen all across Europe in cities, towns and villages. You could look at any given community across Europe and you will find people representing one or other of these worldviews.

But it is not always possible to fit everyone into neatly packaged boxes and often people can be influenced by two or more different worldviews, especially in a multicultural society. However, these categories are nonetheless real. In the Europe of today, there are religious people—Roman Catholics, Orthodox Christians, mainstream Protestants. They believe in God and believe that the church should have influence over their lives. There are Enlightenment Europeans, secular and religiously sceptical. Some are atheists, some agnostics and some who don't take any time to think about religious belief. For them religion is unimportant, and they are guided not by some transcendent religious ethic, but just by what they believe to be rationally acceptable.

There are also postmodern or Emergent Europeans. They are not sure that there is such a thing as objective truth, because truth is whatever you make it. They believe that no one has the right to tell them what to believe or how to live, because that is up to the individual. And there are the new Europeans, the migrant communities. Some are Christian, more are Hindu, Sikh, Animist, and especially Muslim. They are religious and they have their values, but their beliefs and values come, in the main, from religious backgrounds other than Christianity.

This is the new Europe that we as Christians are called upon to reach. If we believe the Great Commission and take it seriously, then we must do something to evangelise this significant area of the world. That job, however, is a formidable one, precisely because Europe is a complex patchwork of cultures and worldviews, with certain important common threads. There are modernists and postmodernists. There are secularists and traditional religious believers, not all of the latter being adherents of Christianity. All, however, are much more influenced by political, social, religious and national traditions than they are inclined to recognise—secular atheists as much as believing Christians. The role of history in forming our identity is characteristic of being European in a much more pronounced way than in some other societies.

Today's Europeans are also very conscious of their Europeanism. Often, they will not only have a commitment to the idea of being European but will even believe that European culture is somehow superior to other cultures, including modern American culture! They do identify with their nationality, whether French, German, Italian, English, Scots, Irish, or whatever. But they also see themselves as Europeans, and this sense of identity has intensified with the recent Russian invasion of Ukraine. This sense of being European may well make Europe a more difficult place to evangelise from outside. Whatever the particular identity and its challenges, all need to be reached with the good news of the gospel.

In the next two chapters, we are going to take a deep dive into European history, both to show why Europe has become so globally influential and also to explain how Europe became the world centre of Christianity, but is now losing its faith fast.

Chapter 2

How Europe conquered the world, and is still influential

We live in times in which we Europeans (and our transatlantic cousins) feel under distinct challenge.

For centuries, perhaps since the first Crusade was declared in 1096, we Europeans have been inclined to see ourselves as having the right and responsibility to direct the world, and certainly to treat the world as a cornucopia whose resources were ours to exploit in our own interests. As early as the eleventh century, western European expansionism began to show itself in the eastern Mediterranean, putting pressure not only on the Saracens in the Levant and Egypt, but also on the Byzantine empire (Orthodox Christians) which was at the same time under a steady programme of conquest by the Seljuk Turks. This led eventually to the fall of Constantinople in 1453, and 250 years of Ottoman advance in the Balkans which reached its high water mark at the gates of Vienna in the sieges of 1529 and 1683, a tide that receded only slowly in the eighteenth and nineteenth centuries and an experience that should never be forgotten when thinking about the Balkans today and mission there.

The thirteenth century also saw European Christian expansion in north-east Europe, where it faced competition from Orthodox Christianity to the south and east. Earlier, between the ninth and twelfth centuries, Catholic Christianity had expanded into Scandinavia, leading to the establishment of archdioceses in Denmark, Norway, and Sweden in the period 1104–64, and, in parallel, Catholic kingdoms in the three countries. There was Catholic missionary work in Finland in the tenth century, and the area was conquered for the Swedish crown in the following century, under whose control it remained until Russian conquest in 1809 (Finland becoming Lutheran along with Sweden at the time of the Reformation, of course).[1] In the ninth and tenth centuries, Catholic Christianity also extended to the Faroes and Iceland.

The medieval mappae mundi (world maps) placed Jerusalem at the centre, but much space in them was taken up with Europe (the mental world maps of Europeans today may not be much different). The medieval maps showed, however, that Europeans were not unconscious that there was a much wider world out there. And from 1450, their expansionary thoughts turned in the direction of that wider world. Their aim was to reach the East Indies, whose spices they had great need for (the Holy Land in the early Middle Ages had straddled key spice routes). But on the way they contacted an Africa whose interior remained hidden to them for another 400 years. With exploration and trade came conquest, by Spain and Portugal in the New World followed by the British in North America, and by the French, Dutch, British and Portuguese in the East, initially more in the interest of control than occupation.

The Hereford Mappa Mundi (map of the world), c. 1300,
the largest known medieval map (though, as it includes
heaven and hell, it is more than a map of the world)

---

1. Finland acquitted itself well when invaded by the Soviet Union in November 1939, though it was eventually obliged to sue for peace in March 1940. It also did relatively well, supported by Germany, in the Continuation War from 1941 to 1944. That Finland so quickly applied for membership of NATO after Russia's invasion of Ukraine in 2022 is easy to understand in the light of history.

Slavery and settlers

For three centuries at least, closely related to the process of colonisation was the transatlantic slave trade between Europe, West Africa and the New World (from which Arabs and Africans profited as well as Europeans). It gave European traders, at least, a particular window on west African society. From the European perspective, the purpose of the trade was to provide slave labour for sugar and rice plantations in the New World, the financial model of which depended on the low cost and farming expertise of slave labour, with all its deeply distressing features. In the longer run, Europe benefitted, including through the capital which was built up and which became significant in funding industrial revolution in Europe from the mid-eighteenth century onwards.

This era was followed in the nineteenth century by extra-European settlement in large numbers, particularly by the British and east-coast Americans but also by other European peoples such as Germans, Scandinavians and Italians into North and South America. As well as settling in the USA, Britons also settled in Canada, South Africa, Australia, New Zealand and Argentina. In all cases, the settlers and their governments viewed the places of settlement less as colonies than as largely vacant lands waiting to support them. At the same time, Russia expanded its empire into the vast vacant territories and unused resources to the east of the Ural mountains, into Siberia and what are now the Stans.

In the late nineteenth century, this process also greatly benefitted the home countries in western Europe through the opening up of cheap sources of food—an important factor in the domestic growth of population and prosperity widely shared across social classes. Europeans saw this settlement process as the occupation and development of empty, backward and, to them, unproductive lands, though that was not necessarily how Amerindians north and south, and indigenous Bantu, Zulus, Australians and Aotearoans (Maoris) saw and experienced it: perhaps understandably, they found it difficult to distinguish between settlers and colonialists.

The nineteenth and twentieth centuries saw the globalization of European power and influence on a scale unknown earlier, especially as the USA should be regarded for these purposes as a European power, certainly as a component of European civilisation (though one prone to bouts of isolationism).

In this context, it should be remembered that, in this era, Europe (and the USA) was essentially a Christianized force and influence (whether Catholic, Protestant, or eastern Orthodox). It is still regarded in this way in many other areas of the world. Many non-Europeans also struggle to understand the secularization of Europe in the last two generations or that European secularism should essentially be understood as a kind of Christian heresy—that is, it maintains a Christianized worldview and ethics, but without their theistic underpinnings. The vast globalization of European power between 1700 and 2000 was not simply a product of the exercise of military power—in many times and places, that was limited; rather, it was often a question of economic, social, cultural, intellectual and religious influence, even of western prestige, and Christian identity and mission played an important part in that.

Backlash, conflict and identity

The fact remains that the extent of European global dominance in the last two centuries should not be underestimated, and it lives on in many places through westernized elites. We should not be surprised at the backlash that it engenders still today in Africa, India, China (proud of its much older imperial civilisation), and across the Islamic world—a backlash that Russia exploits by emphasizing that it is an Asiatic rather than a European power. Nor should we be surprised by the pull of European societies for immigrants from across the world, especially in view of the combination of economic prosperity, and political and social freedom, that characterizes European societies.

We should also remember that, throughout, this process of global expansion was accompanied by intense competition and conflict *between* the European powers, with portions of land outside Europe exchanging hands regularly, particularly sugar plantation islands in the West Indies, the duties on sugar in Europe being important to financing the costly wars that were essential to the process. But the conflict between European countries did not take place simply in far-flung places across the world. It was endemic in Europe from the collapse of the western Roman Empire onwards, and as much between Christian rulers as with non-Christians like Moors, Turks, and Norse—to the distress of the western Catholic Church which sought to contain war between Christians through the beginnings of 'just war' thinking and the 'truce of God' (the latter often unsuccessfully trying to keep the clergy out of warfare).

The early modern and modern eras saw the intensification of conflict between the different European powers which became more ferocious and deadly with technological advance and the advent of a new kind of nationalism which was part and parcel of post-Enlightenment romanticism[2]. The application of modern technology made warfare more catastrophic, for civil populations as much as combatants. But the intensified attachment to national identity (that is, nationalism), coupled sometimes with political ideology, has undoubtedly added to the comprehensive nature of warfare in the modern context: the 'total war' of the two World Wars dragged the whole of society into the conflict.

German troops march past Adolf Hitler, in a
carefully curated event on the banks of the
Vistula in Poland on 16 September 1939

It can be argued that absolute commitment to national identity has in the modern age, in Europe at least, replaced religion as a key source of collective identity and emotional security. This is of particular significance in Europe because of the plethora of national identities that emerged over a millennium within the relatively limited land mass and archipelagos of Europe, at a time

---

2. Pre-modern wars were devastating, less as a result of fighting than through the famine and disease that resulted from the need for armies to live off the land.

when only relatively small political entities were practicable and people's horizons were limited to a single country or even local area. (As late as 1938, Neville Chamberlain could argue that Czechoslovakia was a faraway country of whose quarrel the British knew nothing; in fact, it was only some 650 miles from where he was broadcasting, scarcely further than Inverness.)

It is worth noting here a collective psychological point that is relevant to European attitudes now. The analysis above has emphasized the more or less complete political and economic dominance in the world which Europe (including the UK) gained by the last half of the nineteenth century. Economically, the USA was by then fast catching up with the European powers, with its burgeoning access to resources and rapidly increasing population (thanks largely to immigration from Europe). By the twentieth century, Japan was also beginning to compete economically and militarily. Sometimes we forget the speed with which Europe's dominant position collapsed. This was partly brought about by two bouts of what I have termed Europe's civil wars (WW1 and WW2). But it was also partly brought about by political and philosophical doubt from within about the very idea of empire, a doubt fostered in various quarters of Christian thought since the Reformation and even before. The moral high ground was seized by Marxism in the first half of the twentieth century, calling into question the basis of the whole engine of economic growth in the West.

Whatever the reason, after three centuries of the growth of European power overseas, within a very few years, the commanding European position collapsed. This was traumatic not just for the UK, the most widespread imperial power of all, but for countries like France and the Netherlands which experienced their own rapid retreat from empire. At best, Europe found itself as the acolyte to the USA in half a century of cold war with Russia (as we have argued, both USA and Russia were culturally-speaking part of Europe).

Europe Divided

The cataclysm that Europe experienced in the period 1914–1945 should not be underestimated. The two bouts of intense war in Europe in the early twentieth century produced in the immediate aftermath a wariness about the downsides of enthusiastic national identity in the modern world. Thus the so-called 'European project' (reflected to varying extents in the European Community, NATO, and the Council of Europe) emerged from World War 2 with a three-pronged objective: (1) as a bulwark against an aggrandising Soviet Union (whose practical frontier after the War was across the very centre of Europe), (2) as means of rebuilding Europe's war-depleted economies, and (3) to contain national identities from initiating a third bout of European civil war. The withdrawal of the Soviet Union from eastern Europe to the borders of Russia, and then the collapse of the Soviet Union at the end of 1991, had the effect of extending the boundaries of the European project far to the east and even into the Balkans.

NATO's defence and foreign ministers meet in 2010. It is 75 years since the NATO alliance came into being. Countries bordering Russia remain anxious to join it today.

The immediate wasting-away of Russian state and military power left the focus and priority on building democracy and economies in eastern Europe rather than on defence (it is with hindsight that the neglect of defence comes into focus). The effective removal of external threat left space for concern to be raised about domestic matters and for division within Europe. The post-1990 consensus about political and economic mechanisms in Europe, coupled in due course with economic stagnation after the 2008 financial crash, created circumstances in which, in many European countries, the less well-to-do sensed growing economic insecurity, as well as threat from immigration from eastern Europe and increasingly from outside Europe. In the latter case, this was fuelled not only by the need for labour in an ageing Europe and by the economic attractiveness of Europe, but also by instability in a swathe of countries from North Africa to Pakistan (an instability fomented by high-minded political and military interventionism by the liberal democracies of Europe, America and Australasia).

Europe inherited from its past a system of relatively small states, each with strong national identities, but in many cases with their own opportunities for further splitting, equally based on romantic conceptions of nationalism. Thus Spain (pop. 47.5 m) has strong regional identities, and two separatist nationalist movements, in Catalonia and the Basque country. Italy (pop. 59 m) is divided between north and south, with separatist tendencies in the north. France (pop. 67 m) has a strong tradition of centralised government put in place before and after the Revolution to counteract regional identities, particularly in the west. Belgium (pop. 11.6 m) is deeply split between Flanders on the one hand and Brussels and Wallonia on the other, notwithstanding their historic common Catholicism. The Swiss Confederation (pop. 8.8 m) has French, German and Italian speaking areas and a federal, plebiscitary constitution which leaves much to its 26 individual cantons. Germany (pop. 83.3 m) was divided into some 40 separate sovereign states and cities as late as 1860 and today is a federal state in which the individual *länder* have considerable power; Bavaria and perhaps elsewhere in south Germany still consider themselves distinctly different from the rest of Germany. The sense of being German as an emotional identity remains crucial to maintaining unity at the federal level. The UK (pop. 67 m) is at the same time a highly-centralized state and federated (devolution is recent within Britain[3]). There are three different national identities in Britain (English, Welsh, and Scots) and two in Northern Ireland (Irish and British or more precisely Ulster Scots), and even Cornwall and the Shetlands have pretensions to separate national identity. In England, northerners maintain a strong sense of difference from southerners, and there are enclaves where

---

3. Britain comprises England, Wales and Scotland: hence 'The United Kingdom of Great Britain and Northern Ireland'.

non-Christian religion is an important factor in identity, while in 2021 in London 37% of the population had been born outside the UK.

In central and eastern Europe, this jumbling of different identities in particular states is a common result of the history of the last few centuries. The treaties agreed in 1919 after World War 1 contributed to this: Slovakians were pressed into precarious union with Czechs. Hungary being on the losing side in the War, many Hungarian-speakers north of the Carpathians found themselves citizens of Romania, together with pockets of German speakers. The new Kingdom of Yugoslavia created by the 1919 Peace Conference jumbled together peoples of a variety of identities (as had the Austro-Hungarian Empire before it), and Tito's Marxist internationalism, prestige, and military power continued to hold them together after the Second War. 1990, however, saw comprehensive fragmentation on lines of historic national identity, not without corralling minorities in the 'wrong' country.

The differences between, and the strength and tenacity of, these many different national identities in Europe should not be underestimated, especially as, depending on local political circumstances, politicians in democracies will continue to be unwilling to resist playing the nationalist card when it is necessary to do so. It is not just a question of politics: the legal and administrative traditions of the different countries in Europe, even when based in similar legal systems (whether Roman law or the common law), differ significantly from each other. Traditional approaches to policy problems can also differ notably. These are matters which European integrationists neglect at their peril. When it comes to wider cultural matters the continuing differences between countries become all the more obvious. They must not be neglected in Christian mission, which is the underlying concern of this book. For example, it is not easy for an Englishman to integrate into rural France, and it takes many years, if ever, before mutual understanding develops!

Pulling it all together

Membership of the European Union and of the NATO alliance was (and continues to be) attractive to eastern European states for the economic and defence benefits which they offer, and the Russian invasions of Ukraine in 2014 and 2022 encouraged candidates, for example, in the Balkans and as far distant as Georgia, as well as Sweden and Finland in the case of membership of NATO. This does not mean, however, that there are not reservations about the European Union both among the historic member states and in eastern Europe. With the need to contain conflict between European nation states in mind, the architects of European confederation always intended a united Europe: as the preamble to the Treaty of Rome between the six founder countries in 1957 explained, it was intended as 'a new stage in the process of European integration' in view of 'the historic importance of ending the division of the European continent and the need to create firm bases for the construction of the future Europe' and article 1 of the Maastricht Treaty of 1992 expressed this as 'a new stage in the process of creating an ever closer union between the peoples of Europe'.

It was one thing for the initial six members to state such an objective, especially as they shared common Christian Democratic (i.e., Catholic) traditions of political and social thought. It was another, however, once that tradition became engulfed in the progressive secularism of new generations not only in Protestant north-west Europe but also in Spain and Italy. Today, we can see a clear tension between the progressives in their desire within the institutions of the European Union to use law to advance, as they see it, matters of social practice across the member states on the one hand; and greater social conservatism, particularly in central and eastern Europe, on the other. This is evident in, for example, Hungary, Slovakia, and Poland (this will be unpacked more in chapter 4). To some extent, this reflects the greater residual influence of organised Christianity in eastern Europe, whether Catholic or Orthodox, compared with the western areas of the continent, though, as this text has been finalized for the press in February 2024, the Greek Parliament has defied the Orthodox Church in voting for same-sex marriage..

Layered over this tension is resurgent national identity spread across the European Union as a whole, which expresses itself in populist desire to 'take back control' from remote elites which are seen as controlling the policies of the European Union and restricting the ability of individual member states to resist. This resurgence dates back at least until the 1990s and the Maastricht Treaty which can be interpreted as an example of overreach by those enthusiastic for concentrating power in European institutions at the expense of the traditional powers of member states. This nationalistic populism can now be seen virtually everywhere in Europe, and certainly in recent instances in the Republic of Ireland, Spain, the Netherlands, Sweden, and Italy, though it should be noted that, for the moment, in terms of votes the populists are usually a noisy and significant minority, which the centre and the left are sometimes prepared to combine against in order to keep them out of power.

It should be noted, too, that in many places, the leaders of this populist phenomenon are prepared to argue for the curtailing of the power of courts so that legal process cannot be used to frustrate their populist objectives. To what extent the populists understand the importance of the rule of law within democratic structures, and the limitations that need to be placed on the exercise of executive power, is open to question. When the legal obstruction comes from what seems remote, vaguely understood matters and processes such as the European Convention on Human Rights and the European Court of Human Rights, it is all the easier to use the 'take back control' argument based in the primacy of national self-determination.[4] Where the populist leader is presented as an outsider to the traditional political process, often an established celebrity with an existing public reputation, it seems all the easier for their supporters to trust them with the unfettered power that they would not wish to be conferred on traditional politicians.

Benevolent despotism alive and well in today's Europe

A phenomenon usually associated with Enlightenment Europe is that of 'benevolent' despotism. The European Enlightenment flourished in times before democracy as we now know it was an established form of government (with the exception of the new American Republic and in Revolutionary France in the last decades of the 1700s). The Enlightenment was, however, an enterprise of the very limited educated classes in Europe, and was associated with rulers and a small elite who saw it as their duty to impose virtue on populaces who could not necessarily be trusted to do the right thing. And, unconstrained by public opinion, rulers could do the 'right' thing quicker. Among the educated rulers who have attracted the designation 'benevolent despots' were Frederick

---

4. Institutionally, this is a completely separate matter from the European Union—see Appendix F for a description of key, in most cases, separate European institutions.

the Great of Prussia, Catherine the Great of Russia, and Maria Theresa of Austria and Bohemia and her son, Joseph II. Greatest of all was Napoleon I Bonaparte who, by force of arms, remade Europe on Enlightenment lines. Both Marxism and Gaullism can be seen as continuations of the tradition.

It can be argued that the Enlightenment established a tension between democracy and benevolent despotism, a tension that Europe still lives with. There are many who are disinclined to trust democracy to produce the 'right' results, as they see them, and who seek to use the political process to impose promptly the solutions which they favour. This can be seen in a variety of ways. There is popular support for celebrity rulers who want to limit the power of lawmakers and the courts. At the extreme, the goal may be the establishment of one-party states to achieve preferred ends. But it can also be argued that in democracies, the political lobbying industry (including Christian forms of it) is in essence based on the principle that, by working on and through the system of political institutions, even small minorities can badger decision-makers into doing what the pressure group wants, irrespective of contrary views. This can be anti-democratic and lobby groups can be quite content with that so long as they achieve their purpose. Bible-believing Christians should also recognize their tendency to distrust democracy and inclination to impose virtue on others!

Clearly there is still plenty of benevolent despotism about in today's democracies. Those in power do need to take care how far they should use that power to impose matters on unwilling populations. The great powers of Europe (they still exist) and policy-makers need, for example, to take care how far they should seek to impose contested moral principles on eastern and southern Europe. This is not just a matter for European institutions: the Westminster government and parliament were ready enough to take the chance of the recent prolonged suspension of Stormont to impose matters on what they see as a morally backward population in Northern Ireland. More generally, government in Europe needs genuinely to consult citizens and to be willing to be influenced by their views rather than simply pushing ahead with their own agendas. Another way of putting this is that privilege and special status for some is inherently incompatible with democracy. Today, there are popular movements across Europe that are discontented with top-down, centralist imposition of progressive virtue.

Europe as a Promised Land

We should not ignore two further matters in the European scene.

The first is economic growth in Europe and the economic differences between the different parts of Europe. Even in the past twenty years, Europe has seen significant economic growth, notwithstanding the challenges of the financial difficulties of 2008–9. While, in money terms, nominal GDP per head has doubled or more in Europe overall (and the Scandinavian countries have done rather better than that), the figure has quadrupled or quintupled in eastern Europe (and is 8 – 10 or 11 times higher in Romania, Bulgaria and some of the Balkan countries than it was twenty years ago). So the average standard of living has in relative terms risen twice as much in eastern Europe and the Balkans as in western Europe, perhaps more when account is taken of the fact that the cost of living is lower in eastern Europe than on the western side of the continent.

This growth is no doubt welcome in the countries concerned, and may to some extent be attributable to assistance particularly through membership of the European Union. However, nominal GDP per head is still significantly higher in Western and north-western Europe than in the east and south-east, as shown by the map for 2021 below. For example, predicted GDP per capita in France in 2023 is two and half times greater than that in Romania, and six times greater in the Republic of Ireland and more than five times greater in Norway.

The map for GDP per head, coupled with the democratic and social freedoms of western Europe, underlines why refugees and economic migrants are so anxious to reach western Europe at all costs. It is therefore not surprising that immigration is such a sensitive subject throughout Europe. This has been the case for many years. Since 1950, particular countries have been associated with a particular source or sources, for example, Turkey in the case of Germany, and the West Indies and Pakistan in the case of the UK. In more recent years, serious domestic instability has accelerated migration demand from Afghanistan, Iran, Iraq, and Syria, and more recently from Hong Kong (in the case of the UK) and Ukraine. But differentials of economic growth suggest that generalized pressure from economic migration is likely to be much greater in the future than it has been in the past. This is also true in North America, the demand for immigration being particularly from Latin America. The 'pull' of prosperity, peace, and social freedom in Europe, North America and Australasia should not be underestimated. Nor should the pressure from populations through the ballot box, the social media and other means to reduce immigration be underestimated. In this context, it will be interesting to see how far the longstanding framework of international legal conventions relating to refugees and asylum, and their interpretation, remain unaltered.

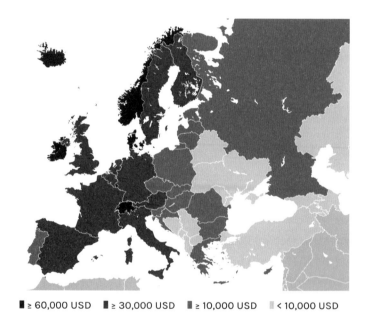

■ ≥ 60,000 USD   ■ ≥ 30,000 USD   ■ ≥ 10,000 USD   ■ < 10,000 USD

European countries by GDP (nominal) per head of population in 2021 (includes transcontinental countries— Russia and Turkey)[5]

5. By Allice Hunter - International Monetary Fund and the World Bank. https://commons.wikimedia.org/w/index.php?curid=109567079

The relevance of religion

The second dimension not to be neglected is that of religion. Those who are attracted to pluralism and secularism tend to neglect, if not denigrate it. There is often the thought underlying pluralism that, fundamentally, religion is unimportant, and therefore that all religions can, or should have, equal standing, and can, or should, be equally ignored. Secularists may go further and regard religion as a vice to be suppressed rather than a virtue. Both ways of thinking lead those who hold them to underestimate the continuing significance of religion in Europe and to propose policies which bring them into significant conflict with important minorities or even, in some situations, majorities. This can be seen by referring to the statistics in Appendix E and noting the high levels of religious commitment in the Catholic and Orthodox countries of southern and eastern Europe, coupled with the rather low levels of those who say that they have no religion (and even something of the same pattern in Lutheran Scandinavia (apart from Sweden)). This being so, we should not be surprised at seeing the societies of southern and eastern Europe showing higher levels of commitment to social conservatism; nor surprised at the presence there of populist leaders who are willing to appeal to those holding such views.

The fingerprint of Europe

Finally, it may be worth noting how Europe has left its style across the world, by exporting key European concepts.

First and most obviously, there is the nation state rooted in national self-determination and underpinned by national identity. This idea was developed in Europe in the early modern period and given a new twist in the Romantic era. But we now live in a world which is universally divided into nation states of this type. These are then brought together by the United Nations, an institution in linear descent from the League of Nations. They are institutions born and developed in Europe. Thanks to the carving out of, mainly, European empires, the boundaries of very many of these nation states follow those of the European colonies which preceded them, boundaries drawn to suit European nations and agreed in European conclaves. As a result, the countries thus created often experience the same kind of internal questions of diverse identity that afflict European states.

Secondly, agreements between the countries of the world are made according to a system of treaties and conventions invented in Europe. Domestic legal systems are largely based on those in Europe, with the exception of some Islamic countries. Commerce and economies follow systems developed in Europe.[6] Concepts of relief and development are still largely those developed over two centuries in Europe. Elites are Europeanized, if only because they are educated in the university, a mode of education which owes its shape to medieval Europe and later responding to industrial revolution there.

So one could go on. Europe may have lost its empires at phenomenal speed. Popular culture may now be a blend of Hollywood and Silicon Valley. But Europe has not lost its ability to project its culture and practice worldwide. In international relations this is a component of what is termed, 'soft power'. Because the UK has withdrawn from the European Union (only one of the supranational structures of Europe), we should not neglect a region of 50 nation states (the gross domestic product of the European Union alone being in excess of £16,000 trillion), which has a continuing cultural influence across the globe.

The arrangements for governmental cooperation in Europe are not well understood by many. For a summary of the main European institutions, including the EU and the Council of Europe, turn to Appendix F.

---

6. The draftsman of this chapter often smiles to himself when he observes in yet another former British colony the characteristic alternately-painted black and white kerb stones.

Chapter 3

How Christianity came to Europe, flourished, and is now at risk

Christianity is not a European invention, though as Islam came to dominate the Levant (the eastern Mediterranean) and the Near East (which were the heartlands of Christianity for the first 600 years of its existence), Europe became its new home. It has been a distinctly European form of Christianity that has been exported across the globe, in the form of Catholicism in the period 1500 to 1750 and evangelical Protestantism thereafter. The plea for help in Macedonia that Paul the apostle experienced at Troas in about AD 49 or 50 (Acts 16: 6–10) has had results of which the recipient can scarcely have conceived. Yet there is real irony, and perhaps judgment, in the fact that, while Europe has been triumphantly successful in taking Christianity to a world of, now, 8 billion people, that same Christian faith is now struggling in the Europe where it had flourished.

Historical retrospective carries the innate danger of concluding that no other pattern of events was possible than those that actually happened, and that what we see today was always so. However, there was no certainty that Christianity would come to dominate European life, west and east. It was not until Constantine adopted Christianity as the emperor's religion in the 320s AD that its foothold became firm in the Roman Empire. It had probably penetrated to all parts before then in a small way, and may even have penetrated a little beyond the frontiers delineated by the Rhine and Danube. But it required official approval to guarantee widespread adoption, an approval that was probably something of a poisoned chalice for the biblical vitality of the faith. Even in the late fourth century, there was an imperial attempt to revert to Roman paganism, and with the economic and military decline of the Roman Empire into the fifth century AD (felt more in the west, that is, Europe, than the east), northern European pagans overran northern and western Europe, to the point of sacking Rome itself in AD 410. Meanwhile, for several centuries the overwhelming centre of gravity of Christianity lay in the east, in the Byzantine empire (which, when Rome was sacked, still had more than a thousand years to run), and in Nestorian Christianity in Armenia and Persia (with missionary activity in the seventh century as far away as in China, Kerala, and Sri Lanka).

In the period AD 400–800, under the leadership of the see of Rome, western Catholicism extended itself through Spain and Gaul, and parts of what is now Germany, though the Rhine and Danube long remained its effective frontier. Its mission extended to Saxon England at the turn of the seventh century, eventually to join up with the separate Celtic mission in Ireland and Scotland. But at the same time, a militant Islam successfully expanded by force of arms into Spain and southern Gaul—and for a period posed a real risk to the future of Christianity beyond the Alps. Only the victory of Charles Martel at Poitiers in 732 stemmed the tide, though it took him some years to clear Muslim forces from the Aquitaine region north of the Pyrenees, and it was to be more than 700 years before Islam was to be fully ejected from the Iberian Peninsula. Charles Martel established the Carolingian dynasty in Francia and the same time pushed east into what is now Germany, cooperating with the missionary work of St Boniface (an Anglo-Saxon from Crediton in Devon in the now-Christian Wessex)[1] and the establishment of monasteries as mission stations. This serves to emphasize the still limited extent of Catholic Christianity north of the Alps in the eighth century, and the extent to which expansion depended not only on missionary work but also on armed authority.

Martel's grandson, Charlemagne, pushed the Frankish kingdom east into Germany and south into Lombardy in northern Italy. The link between church and ruler was underlined when he was crowned Holy Roman Emperor in Rome by Pope Leo III in AD 800.

---

1. Boniface was nevertheless critical of Charles Martel's interference in church matters and property.

Europe at the death of Charlemagne and illustrating
the limited extent of Christianity in both its
western and eastern forms, c. AD 800

We have already noted the steady advance of Catholic Christianity in the early Middle Ages eastwards and northwards in Europe, through the missionary work of clerics and monks, the establishment of bishoprics and archbishoprics, and through the power of the armed nobility. While seeking to bring warfare under ethical conditions, the Christianity of the time and place also celebrated holy war which sanctified military service, especially the crusades from the twelfth century onwards, usually against Islam in the Mediterranean, but sometimes against pagans, as in north-east Europe.

We should not ignore the spiritual fervour that is, from time to time, evident in the pre-Reformation churches. Byzantine Christianity experienced periods of revulsion against the worldliness and wealth of church and society: this was expressed through the desert hermits of the fourth and fifth century Levant, eastern monasticism generally, and eras of extensive iconoclasm similar to that of Puritan England centuries later. Sometimes, these periods of fervour could be sponsored by the political power, whether by kings or their consorts or relatives. There were similar manifestations of fervour and renewal in the western Catholic church in Europe, in the first instance often leading to new monastic orders, some of which were more ascetic than existing orders which had grown wealthy through their industry and the generosity of their sponsors. Later, the revival took the form of the establishment of orders of wandering mendicant friars (religious orders who took vows of poverty and who travelled widely evangelising, especially among the poor—the Franciscans founded by Francis of Assisi, and the Dominicans). These were more involved in society at large than the monastic orders. Spiritual fervour could also manifest itself in the daily domestic religious exercises led by women in well-to-do households.

It could be debated whether any of this spirituality should be regarded as a forerunner of biblical gospel insights recognized in the Reformation, by the puritan and reformed churches that sprang up as widely apart as Scotland, Transylvania and northern Italy following the Reformation, and in the evangelical revivals of the eighteenth century. But we should note that at the turn of the twelfth century Anselm of Canterbury developed the apologetic arguments for the existence of God and added to biblical understanding of the New Testament doctrine of atonement; and that the Cistercian Abbot, Bernard of Clairvaux, wrote hymns which are used by evangelicals today.

What becomes clear as the Middle Ages wore on is that spiritual movements emerged within Catholic Christianity in Europe in widely differing places which anticipated the emphases of the Reformation itself (in a sense, a tribute to the spiritual environment of Catholicism at the time): the Waldensians[2] in the Savoyan Alps who followed Peter Waldo, a merchant who gave up his wealth for poverty in the late twelfth century; the Lollards in early fifteenth-century England; and the Hussites in Bohemia at the same time. In the latter two cases, the original leaders were learned Catholic clergy associated with the universities of Oxford and Prague respectively, who were seeking the renewal of the church. The doctrines of all three groups can be seen to anticipate those emphasized by the reformers in the sixteenth century. There were also the Brethren of the Common Life in the Netherlands (which gave birth to Thomas à Kempis's *Imago Dei* (The Image of God)) and the Dominican Friar, Jerome Savonarola, a teacher of philosophy and a millenarian preacher in Florence in the second half of the fifteenth century.

---

2. The Waldensians still exist today in Piedmont, and include evangelicals among them.

Which leads us to the Reformation and the establishment of Protestantism in Europe.

The European Reformation did not come from nowhere: there were foreshadowings in the previous three centuries as already referred to, and intellectually Renaissance linguistic studies in the second half of the previous century also prepared the way. Many of the early Reformers, including Luther, Zwingli, and Calvin, were part of this new scholarly movement that studied the original languages of Scripture as well as other classical texts. Why the results in the sixteenth century were more dramatic than earlier is harder to explain, especially as the Catholic church in many parts of Europe was less moribund, and had more popular support and commitment, than has sometimes been supposed by Protestants. It is true that Church money-raising efforts, driven from Rome, were widely resented in Germany, and that rulers in northern and western Europe had political and personal reasons to break away from the Catholic church (at a time when the religious commitments of rulers usually determined those of their subjects). The considered commitments of petty aristocrats and landed gentry were also significant in the success of Calvinism in many places—in England, Scotland, France, the northern Netherlands, Poland, Hungary, and Transylvania. These were men rather unwilling to be imposed upon by their superiors. The result was that sovereign territories, particularly in northern and western Europe, quickly adopted the Protestant position: much of northern Germany switched to Lutheranism, as did the Scandinavian kingdoms; the northern provinces of the Netherlands and Scotland became Calvinist. For local reasons, England created a state church which was first Catholic, then one which owed much to the Strasbourg reformation, then Catholic, and then Protestant with, over the years, considerable Calvinist influence. Further south in Europe, there was penetration by the Reformation, including in Spain and Italy. In France, it was so significant that it led in the last 40 years of the 1500s to virtually continuous and debilitating civil war as different noble factions espoused the cause of Catholicism on the one hand and Protestantism on the other. It ended only when Henry of Navarre, the former leader of the Protestants, abandoned them for Catholicism ('Paris is well worth a mass', he said!). In 1598, his Edict of Nantes guaranteed the liberties of the many Protestants in France, but in the following century they were steadily eroded under his son and grandson until the Huguenots were expelled in 1685, to the considerable detriment of the French economy.

In the Netherlands, south Germany, Austria, Hungary, Italy and Spain, Protestants were contending with the deeply Catholic House of Habsburg, led from the mid-1550s by Philip II of Spain. Protestantism was snuffed out in Spain and Italy, hung on by its fingertips in the northern Netherlands and in England by virtue of the early death of the Catholic Queen Mary (wife of Philip II) in 1558 and her succession by her Protestant sister, Elizabeth, who cleverly calculated that English independence would be best served by pursuing a unique form of Protestantism. In the following century, the Austrian Habsburgs initiated the Thirty Years' War from 1620 onwards in Germany. This was devastating, leading to a population reduction of between a third and a half, but had significant success in switching the ruling families of several, mainly south German, states from Protestant to Catholic.

Reformation Wall Geneva

The strength and depth of the Reformation in the sixteenth century was such that it demanded a response by Catholicism, in what has been termed the Counter-Reformation, but which some historians have argued was a form of continued Reformation within the Catholic Church. Certainly, Ignatius de Loyola's own spirituality, and the culture of the Society of Jesus which he founded, could be said to match aspects of Protestantism. But the Council of Trent on the Catholic side, and the various Confessions agreed on the Protestant side, together with the broad territorial standstill reached when the Thirty Years' War ended with the Treaty of Westphalia in 1648, introduced a period of two and half centuries in which Catholicism and Protestantism developed independently of each other. They existed in more or less territorial blocks, with little or no significant influence on each other, except in the importance of differentiating themselves from a caricature of the other.

Catholicism can be argued to have developed in a baroque direction, adopting a form of elaborate religious decoration which we know as baroque and using an elaborate liturgy. Emphasis on Catholic characteristics intensified with a deepening Mariology and veneration of the saints. This also led in the nineteenth century to the declaration, or formalisation, of papal infallibility. The church and clergy enjoyed a high, even dominant, position in society, controlling personal and collective social practice and custom. Yet, compared with Protestantism, there seemed to be a tolerance of shortcomings in political, commercial, and social life. The dominance of the church in many countries led eventually to strong strains of anticlericalism, reflected both politically and in social institutions like the growth of Freemasonry.

By comparison, the character of Protestantism, whatever the form adopted in a particular country, seems to have been altogether more austere and ascetic. This was reflected in the sheer plainness of much ecclesiastical architecture, though in polite society art and music flourished in a restrained but nevertheless baroque manner. In Scandinavia at least (if literature of the nineteenth century is a good guide), the pastor played a strong role in social control of the population, and this may have been the case elsewhere as well. Private enterprise in religion was frowned upon, and in Lutheran Germany preaching was forbidden to those without state recognition at least until the middle of the nineteenth century.

These distinctions continue, even down to the present day in diluted form: visitors in Europe know without too much difficulty whether they are in a country with a Catholic or a Protestant heritage, or an Orthodox heritage for that matter.

Challenge to the religious and institutional status quo

So far, this chapter has been considering institutional Christianity because it was that, closely related to political and military power, which first converted Europe as a whole to the Christian religion. An exception might be the Celtic Christianity of Ireland and Scotland in the mid-sixth century, though that had its connections with Catholic Christianity in the former Gaul. This all began to change with the Reformation, though by then the Waldensians, Lollards, and Hussites (and heretics like the Cathars in thirteenth-century France) had already discovered what it was like to pursue Christian faith outside the confines of the Catholic Church.

The national Protestant churches of the Reformation, whether Lutheran or Calvinist or indeed Zwinglian, did not challenge the medieval assumption, going back to Augustine of Hippo, that the church should be closely related to the state within which it was found, and that all citizens were de facto members of it. Thus, the ruler of a region or country, and his or her religious convictions, were crucial in determining the religion of the particular entity that he or she ruled, whether individual citizens liked it or not. But the Reformation very quickly gave birth to religious communities which challenged this model, immediately in the Anabaptist (later termed Mennonite) congregations which sprang up as early as the 1520s in The Netherlands, Germany, and Switzerland. They were separatist in principle, holding that the ruler should have no control over or connection with churches, and that congregations should be independent, and made up only of committed believers. In the context, this was a revolutionary idea, and they experienced persecution from both Catholics and other Protestants, as the Mennonites continued to do in Europe for three centuries.[3] But it was not long before the notion of the independency of congregations, and freedom from state interference, emerged among Calvinists too, in England in the form of the Brownists towards the end of the sixteenth century. This independency could be seen among paedobaptists

---

3. They suffered, too, from guilt by association with the millenarians of Münster and elsewhere.

(the Congregationalists) and advocates of believer's baptism who had congregations in England by very early in the 1600s. The Wars in Britain and Ireland in the middle of the 1600s accelerated the emergence of separatist groups of Christians, most notably the Quakers (The Society of Friends). The Baptists, Quakers, and others also promoted the notion of democracy, in that their communities were often governed by vote by individual committed members.

There were important developments within Lutheranism in Germany in the seventeenth century which were of even greater significance for the future of Christianity in the world, if not so much in Europe. The Peace of Augsburg of 1555 between the Habsburg Charles V as Holy Roman Emperor and the various princes of the Lutheran Schmalkaldic League (which was a military alliance of Lutheran princes) brought a degree of religious peace to Germany lasting until the beginning of the Thirty Years' War. It gave recognition to Lutheran territories, and allowed for movement of population between territories so as to permit choice of the religious confession under which people wished to live. It therefore gave a formal place to Lutheranism and a secure future in particular jurisdictions. This 'arrival' of Lutheranism broadly coincided with the departure of the first generation of Lutheran reformers, and, in the usual way, initial Reformation fervour began to wane in Lutheranism—fervour for the 'Reform' now passed to the Calvinists and their centre in Geneva. By the seventeenth century, Lutheranism in Germany had become set in its ways, increasingly inactive and with little excitement about the key biblical principles that had energized Luther and his collaborators.

By the mid-seventeenth century, there were those who saw the need for what might now be termed 'spiritual renewal' within German Lutheranism. The threads were brought together in the 1660s by the 30-year old, Philipp Spener, from Alsace and trained in Strasbourg, Geneva and Tübingen where he had come in contact with Calvinists, Waldensians, and a converted Jesuit. He emphasized both the need for personal spiritual experience of Christ and the need for practical evidence of faith. As a pastor in Frankfurt, he used the home group as the vehicle for renewal—a place for deep study of Scripture which would engage, and even be led by, the laity and which would encourage them in practical Christian life. His watchwords were preaching that communicated with ordinary people, holiness rooted in devotional life, and sympathy for the lost.

He set out his scheme in a manifesto in 1675, which was quickly taken up by pastors, not only in Germany, but in the other Lutheran lands of northern Europe. His learnèd opponents in the church mocked the movement as 'Pietism', and squeezed them out of respectable teaching positions in Dresden and Leipzig, leading Spener and August Hermann Francke to create their own university at Halle in 1694. In the process, the residual Moravian (Hussite) church in Saxony was revived, and philanthropic and overseas mission activities created. The movement spread to Britain (renewing John Wesley in 1838 in a Moravian home group in Aldersgate, London) and to Britain's American colonies where, among others, Mennonites who had fled to the New World were touched by renewal and revival.

A. H. Francke's orphan houses and schools, Halle, Germany, c. 1750, built and maintained on the faith principle which subsequently energized much evangelical missionary endeavour.

This was the beginnings of evangelicalism as a renewal and revival movement within Protestantism, leading to successive revivals in the following two centuries and in the twentieth century to Pentecostalism. From these European beginnings, evangelicalism became a worldwide movement of biblical Christianity, now numbering 550 million believers. Nor did Pietism die within German Lutheranism (nor within Scandinavian Lutheranism): up to the twentieth century, there were new waves of Pietist life, in particular in Germany in the early 1800s—termed neo-Pietism by some—which was interesting, if only because George Müller was converted in a Pietist home group as a university student in Halle in 1825 and was to convey Francke's principle of living by faith not only into his own work but also, in the last decades of the 1800s, into the modern evangelical missionary movement.

We can conclude that there would have been no transatlantic revival movements of worldwide significance in the nineteenth century without European and in particular German antecedents.

Pietism was a non- or anti-institutional challenge to a Lutheranism which was solidifying into institutional stasis in the way that traditional denominations do, and perhaps any new spiritual movement tends to do, given time. Pietism emphasized the personal and relational, both towards God and others, and its key mechanism appears to have been informal—the house meeting. It certainly prioritized discipling and discipleship. This set the tone for evangelicalism, a movement which, from the nineteenth century onwards, both multiplied organizations, and questioned and discarded them at will. For what mattered was less the scaffolding of religion than what was going on at the heart, both of the individual and of the community or organization to which they belonged.

The intellectual challenge to today's Christianity

In chronological parallel with the encouraging developments in Protestant Christianity that have just been described were developments which, as they have worked out, present real challenges for Christianity, and real challenges to its actual day-to-day existence in Europe today. They are developments in which the Reformation and its results have played a part. At origin, they have to do with the interplay between the Renaissance and the Reformation, phenomena which were importantly related.

Chronologically, the Renaissance slightly preceded the Reformation, and it was one of the historical conditions which enabled the latter. It is difficult to pinpoint the beginning of any significant cultural movement, and the Renaissance is no exception. Its origins lie in the vibrant Italian city states of the 1300s. We think of it as an artistic and cultural movement above all, but its significance for this chapter lies in the intellectual sphere and in the great technical development of printing which facilitated mass communication (religious and otherwise), at least among readers and those who could be read to. Gutenberg (the first user of a movable type press) himself recognized that Scripture could be produced as never before (giving freedom for individual readers to think for themselves about the meaning and import of Scripture). The Renaissance method also took the scholar back to the classical originals, including the original text to Scripture. It also led people to think about the material world, and the development of key ways of thinking about it, such as mathematics. This was not just for the purposes of making better weapons (which it did do), but also led them to question accepted interpretations of material reality, including of the cosmos.

This latter aspect was in a sense independent of religion, but brought Galileo into conflict with the Catholic church because he proposed a model of the solar system (aided by the development of the telescope) which contradicted the longstanding explanation of the church. Here, there is a contrast between Catholicism and Protestantism, because of the reduced authority of the latter over the individual and because its theology (focussing on Scripture and the salvation story) was less controlling than Catholicism. Protestantism also had an appreciation of creation which encouraged inquiry into it. Whatever the reasons, it was Protestant thinkers, inquirers and experimenters who were prominent in the development of scientific thought and mathematics in the 1600s. On the other hand, as the fervour of Protestant faith cooled into the 1700s and the application of reason became everything (1650–1750 has been dubbed the Age of Reason), the greater latitude for independent opinion in Protestant societies allowed the development of and commitment to alternatives to Christianity, while the hold of Catholicism elsewhere encouraged sceptical reaction not simply among thinkers but more widely in the societies concerned.

While the framework and ethics of eighteenth-century society remained essentially Christian and atheism was comparatively rare, Christian deism (belief in a rather remote deity based on human reason, not revelation) became common, especially among the limited educated classes and the leadership of the established Protestant denominations. This led to developments in philosophy, the humanities, the arts, and the philosophical frameworks of scientific thought which were full of implications for the future, even while evangelical Christianity was at its peak in the nineteenth century. The result was to be the establishment and transmission of new modes of thinking in school education, the growing universities, the arts and literature, and journalism, all of which, by the late twentieth century, were fundamentally hostile to Christianity. In the twentieth century too, this way of thinking was taken up in mass entertainment which, facilitated by radio, film, television, and then the internet, supplanted religion as the communicator of ethical values in society. This did not augur well for religion, particularly as the latter was slow to take up these means of communication (at least in Europe where broadcasting was at first tightly controlled). The dominant ethic that was now emphasized was absolute personal freedom in individual life, whereas moral restraint seemed central to Christianity, especially in matters relating to sexual ethics. The opponents of Christianity have in the past 200 years succeeded in pulling off a notable double coup: to convince society at large that Christianity is scientifically incredible and that its teaching is puritanical and morally unacceptable, because it suggests that there should be limits on humans' freedom to behave as they wish.

The struggles of institutionalized Christianity in today's Europe

Against this intellectual and social background, it is not surprising that Christianity, especially in its more institutionalized forms, should have struggled to maintain itself in Europe. At the same time, there has emerged a new phenomenon (in Europe, and in fact worldwide)—a growing group of people who define themselves as having no religion, whether they are agnostics or atheists. Very rarely in human history have humans in such large numbers denied that they have any religion. Even now, this phenomenon is European in character, not being identifiable (as yet, perhaps) in other areas of the globe apart from those that are European in culture. And even in Europe, it is clear that the phenomenon is much more pronounced in western and northern Europe than it is in eastern Europe.

Both the decline of institutionalized Christianity and the emergence of those who are of no religion can be seen in the figures in Appendix E. This gives figures for the percentage of national populations which identify themselves as Catholic, Protestant, or Orthodox, the percentage who identify as Pentecostal, Charismatic, or Evangelical (proportions overlapping to various extents with the first three), and the percentage who say that they are of no religion. The estimates are given for the years 1900, 1970, 2000, and 2020, which allows changes to be seen in recent history. Thanks to the fact that for the previous 400 years the form of Christianity, whether Catholic, Protestant, or Orthodox, was in practice determined state by state in Europe (and those forms were highly institutionalized), it is possible to determine clear patterns. They differ between northern and western Europe on the one hand and eastern Europe on the other.

In Scandinavia, the dominance (indeed the unique status) of the state Lutheran churches can be seen at the beginning of the last century, as can the extent to which they were evangelical in character, thanks to the influence of Pietism within Lutheranism and revivalism brought back from north America by Swedish and Norwegian emigrants there. Over the following 120 years, identification with the state churches has remained considerable, though this is not necessarily so of church attendance (see below). Levels of no-religion are moderate in these countries, except for Sweden where 32% now identify themselves as being of no religion.

In the midwestern areas of Europe, Catholicism was strong in 1900, except in the UK, Germany and Switzerland, and no religion was miniscule, except in the Czech lands where it was nearly 10%, even then setting a pattern for the following century in which Czechia has remained the front-runner for 'no religion' among these countries—in 2020, the percentage being 64%. In the group as a whole, generally a quarter or a third or more of the population reckon that they have no religion. The Pentecostal-evangelical group is significant only in Britain and Ireland, though the rise from 0.3% in 1900 to 2% today in France is a credit to the focus that France has had in evangelical mission post-1945 and to immigration of evangelicals from Africa.

Turning south, the dominance of Catholicism in Spain, Portugal, Italy and Malta was complete in 1900 and 'no religion' virtually unknown. The populations of these countries still for the most part see themselves as Catholics, though that is not matched in recent years by church attendance (again see below). 'No religion' has made some inroads in the past 50 years, but only in Italy is it yet really significant (at 17% in 2020).

In central and eastern Europe and the Balkans, it depends on history in the particular country whether the commitment of the population is to Catholicism or Orthodoxy, but the figures suggest that populations still identify largely with whichever of the two confessions their country is attached to. And even today levels of 'no religion' are moderate in central or eastern Europe (except for Estonia's 63%), and low in the Balkans. (It is interesting that in eastern Europe levels of 'no religion' were high in 1970 and fell back in most places in 2000, presumably because, in the era of Communist control, the cautious approach was to declare oneself of no religion, while after the 'change' of 1989–90 there was a return to the traditional confession of the country.) Levels of Pentecostal, charismatic or evangelical commitment remain modest in central and eastern Europe, apart from in Romania and Latvia, and very low in the Balkans, demonstrating that the latter is the neediest area of Europe in gospel terms.

To identify with a particular confession for cultural or historical reasons is not necessarily to demonstrate spiritual commitment. In times when church attendance is no longer compulsory, church attendance is one of the measures of Christian commitment. Here Europe, particularly western Europe, does not do well. In Pew Research Center research in the decade 2008–17, the proportions of people who said that they attended church at least weekly were: Sweden 6%; Norway 7%; UK 8%; Germany 10%; France 12%; and Spain 15% (Russia was 7%). This is not surprising, given that, in other Pew research, the proportion of Christians who said that religion was very important in their lives were: Estonia 10%; Finland 12%; Sweden 16%; Denmark 9%; UK 11%;

Germany 12%; France 12%; and Spain 30%. On the eastern side of Europe, the proportions tended to be larger: Poland 32%; Czechia 25%; Italy 16% (Russia also was 16%). These figures contrast with 68% in the USA; 70–80% in South American countries, and 80–90% or more in African countries.[4] The big lesson here is that if someone says they are Catholic, Orthodox or Protestant, it may be a meaningless statement. All they are really saying is that this represents their cultural heritage; it is not necessarily, or perhaps often, an expression of any kind of real faith.

Nowhere in Europe is Christian commitment of any great significance for most people, but that commitment is certainly weaker in the north-western states than in most places in central and eastern Europe (Czechia and Estonia excepted). That, and the restoration of respect for the traditional Christian confessions, whether Catholic or Orthodox, after 1990, help to explain what the intelligentsia and the literati of the north-western states regard as the deplorable social conservatism of central and eastern Europe.

Continuation of political control/oversight of religion in many parts of Europe

A further feature of the recent history of politics and religion in Europe is worthy of note. In Catholic parts, there emerged a distinct popular anti-clericalism, possibly in response to of the close relationship between church and conservative, if not downright reactionary, government in most places. In Orthodox areas, there was also a close relationship between church and state which can be seen clearly in the example of Russia in the nineteenth century and again since the fall of the Soviet Union. And, of course, in the era of Soviet control, the state in most places was officially atheist, and promoted atheism in education and other ways. Religion (de facto in eastern Europe, Christianity) was feared as a source of alternative ideology. Hence, the need to control the state church, and to supervise other religious groups. The same was true in the relatively short fascist eras in the mid-twentieth century. The result in many continental countries was government ministries which managed and controlled religious groups outside the state church. These have often

---

4. The source of the figures in this paragraph is https://www.pewresearch.org/religion/2018/06/13/how-religious-commitment-varies-by-country-among-people-of-all-ages/

survived the disappearance of fascism and state socialism, and are a factor in the lives of the evangelical groups which have emerged or grown since 1945 in many European countries. It can be argued that they are a feature of the tradition of benevolent despotism which emerged from the Enlightenment in Europe, and which has a flourishing after-life wherever elites think it right to use both government and influence to impose their solutions and values when they lack democratic support. By contrast, the supervision of religious groups is deeply foreign to the cultural tradition of British and particularly American evangelicalism with its emphasis on the separation of church and state. However, the supervision of independent religious groups has deep roots in many European countries and the practice needs to be understood and lived with.

In the next chapter, we shall explore some of the cultural tensions that are becoming increasingly evident in Europe today, and reflect on their implications for Christianity.

Chapter 4

Social and cultural tensions

If you have ever owned magnets, you will know that each has a north pole and a south pole. Both poles are capable of attracting, but also repelling. When a north pole meets a south pole there is an attraction, but when that same north pole meets another north pole, the two repel each other.

In recent years, there has emerged in wider Europe two repellent tendencies which are worth reflecting on because they continue to shape this continent. Just as the religious make-up of Europe has changed since the Reformation, so too has the cultural make-up. This is not surprising because one lesson we learn from European history is that religious change does not happen in isolation.

Europeans have often been credited with being open-minded and expressive, free thinkers who enjoy an uninhibited lifestyle. That is certainly the case, but this very freedom which has become a hallmark of European life has recently been supercharged in some parts of Europe through the advent of so-called woke culture, which has exploded onto the scene, especially among the young.

The birth of woke culture

To be fair, woke thinking is not universally present across wider Europe. Many parts of central and eastern Europe remain socially conservative, and even retain a degree of respect for traditional institutions, including religious ones. Nevertheless, there has been an intensification of cultural expression, and woke thinking has become a definite feature of European life.

The meaning of the term 'woke' is slippery. It has developed from post-modernism and continues many of the ambiguities and contradictions of postmodern thinking. Some cultural commentators define 'woke', as having become aware of the plight of marginalised communities. In other words, a person becomes 'woke' when he or she wakes up to the injustices that are at work in wider society. On the surface, this may seem like an attractive feature of cultural life, but there is another side to the coin.

Woke culture has developed quickly into angry protest movements, in which the social justice warriors at the forefront make extreme claims about the many faults of life in Europe and the West, and try to unpick the very social fabric that has underpinned European life. For this reason, some have labelled woke thinking as Marxist, though this is only partly true. Marx himself was an empiricist who believed in the ideals of community, while woke thinking is both highly individualistic and often lacking in rationality. However, it carries within it the Marxist desire to pull down existing society and rebuild it in a radically different way.

Lying behind woke culture is an intellectual movement which has taken hold in many of Europe's great universities and is often termed, Critical Theory. It can particularly be seen in liberal arts faculties and applies postmodernist thought to a whole range of academic disciplines. For example, it has led to the development of so-called Postcolonial Theory, which seeks to paint the West as a bully that colonised the global South, robbing it of its resources and enslaving its people. While there is historical truth in this claim, the great European colonising powers were not alone in doing so, and the accusation that European powers only harmed and never made a positive contribution is a bit of a stretch.

Critical Theory also stands behind the development of Queer Theory, which tries to banish sexual norms in order to allow freedom not only to live as you want, but also be what you want to be, irrespective of the limitations arising from, for example, biological realities. A subset of Queer Theory is Gender Studies which deliberately blurs the distinction between genders and rejects the 'binary' categorisation of male and female, perceiving them to be artificial categories imposed by society, rather than being factual physical distinctions between human beings. Working in tandem with these is Critical Race Theory which sees racism everywhere, and insists that European and indeed all Western societies have institutionalised racism and perpetrate racial injustice as the norm.

These scholars are frequently propagandists who want to change society. This can be seen in selectivity with respect to evidence, denial of biological reality, and conclusions which are often devoid of logic and angry in tone. The penetration of this kind of thinking, especially in many of Europe's universities, non-governmental and other institutions is significant. Given that this continent is home to social conservatives as well as religious communities, it is also highly divisive.

Who would have thought a few generations ago that we would come to a point in our cultural history at which intelligent and highly educated people struggle to define what a woman is? Who would have imagined that people who have grown up benefitting from the security and privilege that European life offers denounce Europe as an evil bully and slave trader, while turning a blind eye to the injustices perpetrated in other parts of the world? Moreover, who would have thought that we would arrive at a point in European history when privileged and educated Europeans would de-platform, silence and insult people who don't agree with them, all in the name of freedom and justice. This is the Europe of woke culture.

All of this has contributed to the ferment that is Europe today. Protest has become a fixed part of our culture. Woke movements are aggressive and increasingly disrespectful of the law. Something of this could be seen in the pulling down of the statue of Edward Colston of Bristol which had stood for 125 years in the city centre. It was torn off its plinth by a mob who then dropped it into Bristol harbour because Colston's wealth was acquired in the late 1600s from the slave trade.

It can be seen in the so-called Margot case in Poland, where a male activist who identified as a woman was arrested for an attack on pro-lifers who were passing a group of supporters of the Polish pro-choice movement[1]. Those who opposed Margot's demand to be sent to a women's prison were vilified and in some cases sent death threats. This was not an isolated case, as much the same happened in Scotland when Isla Bryson, a biological male charged with

---

1. https://europeanconservative.com/articles/essay/the-woke-revolution-isnt-by-passing-poland/

A nineteenth century statue of Edward Colston is
consigned to Bristol harbour during a protest in 2020.
Colston was a Bristol-based merchant and deputy
governor of the Royal African Company, which held the
British monopoly in trade with west Africa, including
of slaves; he was a benefactor of Bristol, as well as its
MP from 1710–13. His name has been expunged from
a number of institutions and activities in Bristol.

rape, was initially sent to a women's prison[2]. Woke culture was evident in the
Miss Netherlands pageant in 2023 when the winner, Rikkie Valerie Kolle,
was a transgender woman who was born male[3]. She went on to represent the
Netherlands in the Miss Universe competition. Woke culture can also be seen
in the trans debate in which institutions are competing to name an increasingly
large number of genders (the American School in London posits 64 genders,
Facebook 71 genders, and the BBC 100 genders).

Woke culture can be seen in 'cancel culture'. Universities, which are
supposedly meant to be places of free thought and debate, are now being

2. https://en.wikipedia.org/wiki/Isla_Bryson_case#:~:text=The%20case%20caused%20
controversy%20after,transferred%20to%20a%20male%20prison.

3. https://www.nbcnews.com/nbc-out/nbc-out-proud/trans-model-actress-crowned-miss-
netherlands-will-compete-miss-univers-rcna93554

pressurised, often by their students, into censoring opinions that are perceived to be harmful. This form of ostracism closes down debate, suppresses free speech and even prevents opposing views from being sifted in a quest for truth. It is not dissimilar to the quest for 'safe spaces' where those with apparently delicate ears are sheltered from something that they may not approve of or find too challenging. This is of concern to Christians because, if everything is carefully filtered, we may come to the point that we cannot freely preach the gospel or even teach the Bible faithfully in our church services.

Woke culture can be seen, too, in some of the green agenda. Many green activists are not so much in love with nature as they are opposed to capitalism. They want to tear down much of the social fabric of the West and usher in a new world that does not recognise the importance of a Creator to whom we owe loyalty. Again, this aspect of woke culture has little respect for social norms. The campaigners who block roads during the Tour de France, throw soup over iconic works of art, or stage sit-ins at major airports like Schiphol in Amsterdam, have little concern for the rule of law and show a disregard for democracy, as they assume that their own moral sense outweighs all else. Even the highly effective communicator, Greta Thunberg, seems not to wish to contribute positively to the formal political process, but campaigns and protests by other means.

It would be wrong to conclude that Europe as a whole is 'woke' just because a proportion of its population is vocally so. The truth is that woke culture grabs the headlines, partly by shouting loudly and partly because reporting conflict sells newspapers and attracts TV viewers. But there is a reaction to woke thinking that reverberates around Europe. For example, when Giorgia Meloni was campaigning to become Italian Prime Minister in 2022, she made social values a clear part of her agenda, as she spoke against what she described as the 'European progressive mainstream'. She openly expressed her opposition to abortion, euthanasia, same-sex marriage and transgenderism. In a speech that went viral, she boldly declared, 'I am Giorgia, I am a woman, I am a mother, I am Italian, I am Christian! You won't take it from me'.[4]

---

4. https://www.youtube.com/watch?v=PXocFMRtBQk

Giorgia Meloni, a conservative populist and first female Prime Minister of Italy following the victory of a centre-right coalition in the election of October 2022.

Victor Orban, Prime Minister of Hungary, is someone who likewise opposes woke progressivism. And he has been outspoken about the dangers of separating western civilisation from its Judaeo-Christian roots and has argued that the most evil acts that have been committed in Europe have been carried out by people who have opposed Christianity.

It is not just the conservative Christian right that has expressed opposition to woke thinking. Europe's large and growing Muslim population is also opposed. As around a dozen European countries have Muslim populations of 5% and growing, this is hardly surprising. There is a range of opinion among Muslims from liberals all the way to fundamentalists. However, Muslims in general are more socially conservative than their fellow Europeans and many of the woke values being espoused by activists are strongly condemned by leading Muslim teachers.

All this means that Europe is a conflicted place. Progressive liberals who are often buoyed along by woke activists find themselves in opposition to traditionalists and conservatives, whether religious of not. Nevertheless, the voice of woke liberalism is strong and has certainly made significant inroads in both politics and education. This means that the values that woke culture espouses will be here for a long time and so will the conflict with those who think differently. This will add to the confusion that is part of European life and shapes the atmosphere within which Europe's children will grow.

The rise of populism

Woke culture encounters a repellent force in populist nationalism.

We should recall that democracy is actually a relative newcomer to Europe, and one that is still surprisingly fragile. Universal suffrage, the right of all adults to vote, was only introduced into western European countries after World War 1. In eastern European countries, democracy was mainly snuffed out after 1918, and again very soon after World War 2, and it was not properly restored until after 1990. The front runners of democracy were the UK, France, and Germany who began this form of political life in the nineteenth century, and in the case of France after 1789. (We should note that some form of voting for governments was present in some cities in Europe in the Middle Ages, mostly in Italy, but was often manipulated by rulers and others who intimidated voters.)

Democracy in Europe (including essential features such as the rule of law and the role of the courts) is therefore a young and tender plant, especially in eastern Europe and the Balkans. Given its vulnerability, it is perhaps not surprising that it has been challenged by populist leaders in many parts of Europe. This has manifested itself especially in France with Marine Le Pen, the Netherlands with Geert Wilders, Italy with Silvio Berlusconi and then Giorgia Meloni, Hungary with Viktor Orban, Poland with Jaroslaw Kaczynski, Sweden with Jimmie Akesson and also the UK with Boris Johnson, Richard Tice (the leader of Reform UK) and Nigel Farage.

There are many reasons for the rise of populism. First, with the prominence of European institutions such as the EU, many have come to the conclusion that Europe is a club for elites. These elites are believed to be self-serving and happy for resources to flow towards the already well-to-do. It means that the rich and privileged get richer while others get 'left behind' economically, culturally and psychologically (notwithstanding the efforts of the EU Structural and Investment Funds).

Secondly, there is the belief that these same elites have introduced their own morality, including around the issues of gender and identity, and that this new morality is radically different from that which many ordinary Europeans believe in. It is particularly here where populism comes into direct conflict with woke ideology. Many populist leaders argue that these new liberal values are being imposed upon a population from above (in effect, as a project of 'benevolent' despotism) and no one is being asked what they think about the issue.

Thirdly, there is the question of control. European political institutions pass laws which are often unpopular and which are perceived to be restrictive of personal freedoms. This is seen as government interference in the lives of individuals and is particularly objected to in a European context when it is perceived that these rules are being handed down by unelected bureaucrats.

Fourthly, there is the question of immigration which many Europeans believe to be uncontrolled and perhaps even uncontrollable. Some politicians, and certainly businesses, are relaxed about migration in order to fill job vacancies (e.g., in the UK in the health service, transport and agriculture). Some may be philosophically committed to multiculturalism and unconcerned about the increasing diversity of Europe. However, populists argue that these migrants are not only taking jobs, keeping wage rates down, and absorbing too great a proportion of already stretched public services, but that they are also changing the very nature of local communities. While migrants are often the most dynamic, energetic and competent from the societies that they are leaving, they are still seen as not adding value to wider society, despite the fact that those with, for example, Indian and Chinese backgrounds are often very successful because they are competent in business and committed to educational success in their children. This very success may sometimes stir up a sense among native Europeans that they are being elbowed aside.

Fifthly, there is a collective forgetfulness about the dangers of nationalism, which had disastrous consequences for Europe in the recent past. The level of international cooperation today is astounding compared with that at the end of the nineteenth century—all underpinned by numerous treaties and enforcement mechanisms. Much of this is beneficial and necessary, and we scarcely notice it. But there is now little memory and appreciation of the horrors into which the different nationalisms of Europe led in the first half of the twentieth century, how bad that was, and what havoc those nationalisms could still wreak (though the invasion of Ukraine may be waking us up to it and we ought to remember what happened in the Balkans in the very recent past).

Finally, there is the threat to national identity and with it a loss of sense of security in a rapidly changing world. This includes a loss of traditional sources of individual and collective identity, including religion and a nation's cultural values. The fear is that regional and national identity is being suppressed through politically driven multiculturalism. But in an insecure world, especially one in which few think God has serious concern for it and them, people turn to national and cultural identities as a substitute for finding identity in God. This is only a short step from idolizing the nation state and populist leaders.

What is it that populist leaders offer that is so appealing? In part, it is their celebrity status. They are often dynamic and charismatic figures who are skilful at courting the press and therefore become very high profile. They also cleverly cast themselves as being against the established elites and, therefore, they are more often than not seen as 'one of us' or a 'man of the people'. Given that some populist leaders, such as the late Silvio Berlusconi, Boris Johnson, Nigel Farage, and especially Donald Trump in the USA, are actually privately educated, upper middle class, hugely successful and often very wealthy, this is somewhat ironic. It nevertheless demonstrates their communication ability when they can present an empathetic front which appeals to people who are in the 'left behind' category. Often they gain this popularity by saying things publicly that others believe, but would not dare say (including on issues of morality), things the cultural elites would disagree with.

The populist leaders also present themselves as saviour figures, the louder and more bombastic the better electorally. They promise to restore the economic fortunes and social status of the 'left behinds'. They promise to secure borders and to protect indigenous cultures from outside influence, exciting national pride in the process. All the while, they present themselves as heroic figures in whom their followers can take vicarious satisfaction. There is also an attempt to play some sort of prophetic role, denouncing all the wrongs that they see, speaking for the underdog, and warning of the doom to come if government policy doesn't change.

All of this is helped by the fact that they tend to be often excellent, simple communicators, skilled in a range of communication methods (including social media), and presenting a persona that is the opposite of the caricature of a dull politician. Volodymyr Zelenskyy is a particularly interesting example of this, given that he was an actor and comedian before entering politics. He is an excellent communicator with the spoken word on TV and through social media. Even his appearing in simple, unadorned military style clothing, rather than a suit and tie, communicates a man of action and conveys that he identifies with the common soldier who is bearing the brunt of battle. At the same time, it differentiates him from the elite whom many suspect of gaining, perhaps illegitimately, from their status.

Populist leaders are also unafraid to argue against the knowledge of intellectuals and experts. This plays well with an audience that has become cynical about what the experts apparently know. Refuge is also taken in romantic fantasies about past, golden ages when things were so much better. At the extreme, there is resort to fantasies and conspiracy theories, which are to be believed precisely because they do not come from intellectual or social elites with the rigorous verification that is required in those circles.

Populist leaders also get things done! It was said of the fascist dictators of the 1930s that they made the trains run on time, and this was used by their supporters as justification of their rule. The same is true of today's populists who are quite prepared to smash down barriers like parliamentary constraints, the rule of law and 'obstructive' judges, in order to achieve their goals; and their supporters admire them all the more for it. They are often 'macho' figures whom their male followers identify with (and perhaps some of their female followers are attracted to). An interesting exception is Giorgia Meloni who is a prominent but female populist leader, but nevertheless one who is highly charismatic and outspoken.

Some populist leaders have been guilty of questionable and even outrageous behaviour, but this does not seem to be a barrier to electoral success and is even justified on the basis that they are a living embodiment of libertarianism, whereas their elitist opponents are controlling and illiberal.

One interesting feature of populism is that it has proved attractive to some evangelicals, even when the populist leader does not conform to biblical morality, especially in the all-important (for evangelicals) aspect of sexual morality. Populist nationalists appear to be on the side of the small, marginalized person, and that is where many evangelical Christians also position themselves. Moreover, evangelicals see themselves as social outsiders and they too are concerned with the moral tone set by the elites, just like the populists. Most populist nationalists at least present themselves as social conservatives who align themselves with Europe's Christian past and make overtures towards supporters of traditional Christian religion and morality, and are therefore seen as preferable to atheistic secularists who seem to predominate among the elites.

Navigating culture

As we reflect on the presence of these two mutually repellent forces in European culture, we need to ask the question, how should we as evangelicals relate to these two groupings? What should our attitude to them be and how should we navigate our way through this complex cultural setting?

Perhaps the first thing we should do is to acknowledge that some evangelicals, in the USA at least, naturally lean towards the populists because of their emphasis on traditional morality. Herein lies a danger because, while we do have something in common with populist agendas, we still need to be wise in the way we relate to populism and not become too closely aligned with it. Remember, we are all fallible human beings and, while there are things to commend the views of some populist leaders, they have their faults too and we should not be blind to them. This is not simply a question of concern about their celebrity style and personal morality. If we value democracy as a way of government[5]—not only a matter of the sovereignty of the people

---

5. Democracy is not, of course, the biblically advocated form of human government. Perhaps the clearest point in Scripture on the matter is that all de facto government, whatever its constitutional form, virtue and vices in the particular case, is ordained of God and to be given due respect by Christians, even when it lapses into tyranny and persecution (when it may need to be resisted at least passively, as the book of Revelation abundantly suggests). However, democracy has its roots in Christianity (as well as in some of the Greek city states of antiquity)—the

in the ballot box (which itself needs protection from politicians in power), but checks and balances such as the rule of law, the independence of judges, and freedom of the press and expression more generally, then we do well to be cautious, in the light of evidence as widely spread as the USA, the UK, Hungary, Poland, Russia, and Israel. The risks that populists will seek to use their majority in the legislature (when they have it) to interfere with the checks and balances that secure democracy in the long-term are real. We also need to beware of the very common human argument that the end justifies the means. Just because a populist leader will advocate some traditional moral positions, that should not blind us to their own personal fallenness or indeed other policies of theirs which are equally immoral or regrettable. What is more, as Paul reminds us in Ephesians 6:12, 'our battle is not against flesh and blood but against principalities and powers.' While we may support the populist tendency to push for traditional morality in society, what our culture really needs is the transformation that is brought about through the gospel. It is on the life-changing message of Christianity that we should pin our hopes.

This is not to say that we should avoid political involvement; quite the reverse because we should be salt and light everywhere, including in the political realm. But any political involvement should be accompanied by an integrity of life, as well as a commitment to sharing a living faith that is built on the foundation of a Christian worldview.

This said, we still need to navigate through these two opposing cultural forces. The best way to do so is to be 'Wise as serpents and harmless as doves' (Mt. 10: 16). In many contexts for the Christian in mission, that will involve not taking sides or passing judgment, but rather looking for ways of building bridges to both groups, while remaining sufficiently detached so as not to become defined as being in either camp.

In the case of woke culture, it will mean recognising that it has some foundations that we can build on. The key connecting point is our common interest in social justice. At the heart of woke culture is the fact that in society

---

eventually unique bishops of the city churches in the Roman Empire were elected, and we have already referred to government by vote in some congregational-type churches in Protestantism. More pragmatically, the evidence is that human rights, individual liberty, and restraints on the abuse of political power, are safer under democratic forms of government than the alternatives.

there are winners and losers, and that we live in a world where some are discriminated against. This fight for justice takes a stand against racism, which is clearly an evil. It expresses concern for ethnic minorities who may face derision and prejudice, and whose life opportunities may sometimes be more restricted than those of the dominant ethnic group. It is also concerned about sexism, misogyny, and the mistreatment of people based on their gender or lifestyle. It demonstrates concern for the poor and the marginalised, as well as opposing exploitation by powerful nations (including Russia and China) and dominant multinational companies.

Cries for social justice fit well with the Christian concern for justice. In Luke 4, Jesus is recorded as reading from the book of Isaiah these famous words:

> [18] "The Spirit of the Lord is on me,
>   because he has anointed me
>   to proclaim good news to the poor.
> He has sent me to proclaim freedom for the prisoners
>   and recovery of sight for the blind,
> to set the oppressed free,
> [19]   to proclaim the year of the Lord's favour."

Having finished reading the passage, he declared, 'Today this scripture is fulfilled in your hearing' (v. 21). His ministry was about bringing the good news to a broken world, and part of that mission was to stand for social justice. It is here that the Christian message can be seen to be relevant everywhere in Europe today. When we as Christians express the desire to condemn and stop bullying, bigotry, prejudice and manipulation, when we stand up for the poor, the marginalised and the oppressed and seek to meet their needs when we can do so, we act in a way that can connect with culture.

That is not to say that we should uncritically accept everything in culture: we should evaluate it and be concerned about aspects of woke culture that are anti-Christian. We should bear in mind that the foundation of woke morality is not the Bible. That does not make all its moral instincts wrong, for after all, we are made in the image of God, and many principles of secularist culture in fact owe their origins to Judaeo-Christian thought. Fallen and flawed people can have a genuine sense of what ought to be, a sense that can be superior to that of religious people, as the apostle Paul recognized in Romans 2: 13–16. However, a morality not grounded in the biblical revelation will inevitably be a pale reflection of the real thing.

We should also be careful about the tendency within woke thought to impose itself on others and to be highly illiberal ('benevolent' despotism again). Christians should be advocates of free speech. After all, if culture gets to the point where unpalatable voices are repressed, we may find that we no longer have the freedom to preach the gospel or biblical truth. Our freedom is the freedom of all.

Much the same attitude should be shown to populists on the right. We should recognise and applaud their commitment, even if merely a matter of temporary political convenience, to upholding traditional moral values. These should be affirmed, and we should express appreciation and support for their efforts. We should also recognise that often populists express genuine appreciation for the church and the Christian legacy, and oppose attempts to push the Christian faith to one side. Yet at the same time we recognise that spiritual objectives cannot be achieved through civic power. Our society will not get better simply by passing new laws. Rather it will be transformed one person at a time, as individuals surrender to the lordship of Christ and then cooperate with others in the fellowship of Christ. Our focus should not so much be on supporting populist political causes, but on gospel proclamation and doing the works of the Kingdom.

Let us take stock of what we have covered so far. We have taken a deep dive into European history, politics, religious belief and culture. We hope that by now you will see that Europe is certainly a deeply complex place, with many layers that need to be explored so that understanding can shape our mission work. What does all of this mean for the proclamation of the gospel? In the next chapter, we shall take a whistle-stop tour of wider Europe, to see where the spiritual needs lie.

Chapter 5

The spiritual needs of Europe

Having thought about the kind of place Europe is, we now need to reflect on the different areas of Europe and ask what spiritual needs exist? Allow us to be your tour guide as we take a bird's eye view of the spiritual needs of this fascinating region.

The Scandinavian North

We begin with Scandinavia which many believe to be one of the most prosperous and desirable parts of Europe. **Norway** and **Iceland** are not members of the EU, but share a Viking ancestry with **Denmark** and **Sweden**. **Finland** was part of Sweden for centuries until 1809, while Iceland only became independent from Denmark in 1944.

Scandinavia's history has been varied. During the time of King Canute, Norway, Sweden and England were under Danish rule. In the thirteenth century, parts of Scotland were under Norwegian rule, while Finland fell to the Russians in 1809 and, as the Grand Duchy of Finland, remained under Russian control until the collapse of the Russian Empire in 1917. During World War 2, Sweden remained neutral, while Denmark and Norway fought the Germans in resistance movements of varying strengths.

The Scandinavian countries are nominally among the most Christian in Europe. The State Churches are Lutheran and enjoy high membership. Most members pay the (optional) taxes which support the churches. However, these facts mask serious spiritual problems. A combination of liberalism, secularism and apathy means that Scandinavia is spiritually needy. In **Denmark**, for example, 90% of the population are members of the Lutheran Church and 50% say that they pray regularly, but most parishes have church attendance of between 1% and 4%. Likewise in **Sweden**, while 78% of the population were baptised as infants into the Lutheran Church, less than half believe there is a God and only 5% go to church. In the nineteenth century, Sweden enjoyed evangelical revivals (encouraged by links with Swedish emigrants to north America), a vigorous Free Church movement, and a huge interest in mission. The past century has led to secularism and one of the most permissive cultures in the world. There is some evangelical growth, particularly among Charismatic and Pentecostal churches (the Pentecostal Alliance of Independent Churches alone has 430 churches with 85,000 members), but the need is greater than ever.

Norway is more encouraging. It has been one of the world's great missionary-sending nations and the influence of Pietism has been significant for the past two centuries. The State Church has many evangelical pastors, though they battle with their liberal counterparts who have campaigned for and achieved same-sex marriage in the church.[1] The free churches are numerous, often vibrant and committed to church-planting.

Finland is a country of contrasts. Secular humanism has had a huge influence on the national psyche, with two thirds of Finns believing that life is devoid of hope. However, there are many evangelicals within the state church and while free churches are small in number, many are vibrant and growing. Commitment and fragmentation remain persistent problems.

Iceland has the smallest percentage of evangelicals in Scandinavia. Most state church members are nominal and the pastorate often liberal. New Age ideologies and the occult are common. There is the general moral decline and disintegration of society. The main evangelical thrust comes from Pentecostal and charismatic churches which are endeavouring to church plant.

Greenland has a land mass eight times the size of the United Kingdom but a population of 56,500, roughly the same as Torquay (south west England), Poprad (Slovakia), or Vannes (Brittany, France). Though linked to Denmark, Greenland is self-governing, and its population comprises mostly Inuit peoples, who are traditionally shamanistic. Life on this inhospitable island is challenging, and there are high levels of immorality, alcoholism and suicide. Many

---

1. https://www.reuters.com/article/us-norway-gaymarriage-idUSKBN15E1O2

villages have a Lutheran church, but these are mostly empty. Evangelicalism has only existed in Greenland for half a century (though earlier there was Pietistic and Moravian influence) and there is a great need for indigenous leadership; however, there are some signs of growth.

The seventeen inhabited islands of the **Faroes** are the most Christian part of Scandinavia. This Danish territory, self-ruled since 1948, has a population of around 454,000 of whom evangelicals comprise 29%. There is a lack of trained leadership and structure, but churches are mission-minded. There are evangelicals within the Lutheran State Church, though most members are nominal Christians. Most evangelicals are Brethren, and these churches have shown consistent growth over the past century.

COUNTRY	POPULATION	% EVANGELICAL[2]
Denmark	5,932,654	3.5
Faroes	54,255	28.8
Finland	5,538,238	12.1
Greenland	56,446	4.7
Iceland	390,830	3.8
Norway	5,434,319	8.4
Sweden	10,521,556	6.9

The Mid-West

We turn to the Mid-West, a diverse group of nations tied together by history and culture. We begin this part of the tour with the islands of the **United Kingdom** (UK) and Ireland. The United Kingdom unites Great Britain (England, Scotland and Wales) and Northern Ireland. These are individual countries in their own right, each with a sense of their own identity, but united as a single kingdom (but with varying measures of devolution to Scotland, Wales and Northern Ireland).

The UK was formed in 1801 as a Union of Great Britain (a united kingdom between 1707 and 1801) and Ireland. The Republic of Ireland was recognised as a separate state in 1922. Even before 1707, the countries of the UK played a significant role on the world scene. The British Empire once covered one quarter of the globe and today the Commonwealth comprises 54 member states

2. These figures, and those in the other tables in this chapter, are as given in the 2010 edition of *Operation World*.

with a population of 2.4 billion (three member states—Gabon, Mozambique, and Rwanda—not having been part of the British Empire). The UK was the first industrialised economy and still ranks as the fifth largest economy in the world. It has also been a centre for democracy and human rights, paving the way for the parliamentary system of government and constitutional monarchy.

The United Kingdom has been primarily Protestant since the reign of Henry VIII (1509–1547). The Church of England (Anglican) is the church established by law in England[3] and the Church of Scotland (Presbyterian) is recognised by law as the national church in Scotland. The UK has been blessed with revivals and great Christian leaders and has been a key centre of Christianity and mission for the past two centuries. However, Christianity is in decline and in the 2021 census only 46% of people in England and Wales identified their religion as Christian. Moreover, the UK as a whole needs a new sense of direction, especially in the aftermath of Brexit, COVID, government scandals, and the ongoing moral decline that began with the 'flapper' generation after WW1, the upheavals of WW2, and the 'freedoms' of the 1960s. There are alarming levels of alcohol and drug abuse, sexually transmitted diseases, abortion, and personal debt. The Judaeo-Christian worldview which was held almost universally by people up to 1900 is now almost totally eroded.

Overall, evangelicals are holding their own, but only because of migration. Most growth is happening within Pentecostalism and the New Church movements. Perhaps the most exciting development has been the growth in black majority churches, helped by the large numbers of Christians among the population of Caribbean and African immigrants and their descendants born in the UK. There has been growth in church attendance in London, where 37% of the population in 2021 was foreign-born. Unfortunately, while many black majority churches are relevant to their own communities, they are not succeeding in reaching out to society at large, and that society may in general be unwilling to hear any message for this source. As many as 25% of black communities are churchgoers and many identify with culturally conservative Pentecostalism.

---

3. The Church of Ireland and the Church in Wales were at one time established by law in those territories, but the Church of Ireland was disestablished in 1868 and the Church in Wales in 1920 by legislation of 1914, the implementation of which was delayed by WW1.

The Church of England is parent to 81 million Anglicans worldwide and it encompasses evangelicals, liberals and Anglo-Catholics. The result is that there are divisions over questions such as homosexuality, the ordination of women, and the attitude towards the Roman Catholic Church. Evangelicals have been a growing force within the Anglican churches in the UK and represent 34% of church attenders. Charismatics have also contributed to a renewal process which may well, in time, change the Church of England.

Although people in the UK are among the most religiously cynical in Europe, there are some signs of hope. Many evangelicals have been able to adapt to changing culture and there is now evidence of creativity in evangelism and flexibility in church life. Initiatives like the Alpha course have been significant and many churches use it. That said, many evangelical congregations are still in decline.

The Republic of Ireland has a very different history and virtually since the Reformation there was conflict between Protestant Britain and Catholic Ireland which has accentuated Irish self-identity. In the twelfth century, Anglo-Norman nobles invaded Ireland and were eventually assimilated into Irish society. Then in the early seventeenth century, large numbers of particularly Scottish Protestants settled in north-east Ireland causing conflict. In 1649–53, the Catholic forces were brutally crushed by Oliver Cromwell, once he had prevailed in the civil war in England.

Monarchy was restored in Britain and Ireland in 1660, and in 1685 a Roman Catholic, James II, succeeded his brother and gave hope to Irish Catholics. When James II was deposed by the Protestant, William of Orange, James went to Ireland to raise an army against the new Protestant rulers. He was defeated by William of Orange, who is hailed to this day as a saviour by Protestants in Northern Ireland. Eventually after suffering two centuries of widespread discrimination and famine, Ireland was partitioned in 1922 by Act of Parliament which gave birth to the predominantly Catholic Republic of Ireland.

Today, Irish people are keenly aware of their history and identity. However, there is no official link between the Roman Catholic Church and the Irish state; and, in general, the church's influence, though once strong, is on the wane— not least because of sex-abuse scandals and cover-ups and the rapid growth of secularism in Ireland, reflected in popular decisions on same-sex marriage and the relaxation of abortion laws.[4] Ireland has become wealthy, helped by its privileged position within the EU. It can be argued that the main reason why Irish people today do not convert to evangelical Christianity in large numbers is not because of their allegiance to the Catholic Church, but rather their materialistic lifestyles coupled with the penetration of secularist thought.

Nevertheless, despite this apathy, there are signs of life. The Charismatic movement has had a significant impact on the nation. Many of these charismatic Christians are within the Roman Catholic Church, but they show increased interest in the Bible and in personal spirituality. Within the Protestant tradition in the Republic, there has been slow but steady growth of evangelicalism. This can particularly be seen in the mainline Pentecostal denominations and in the many small independent fellowships across the country. There is still much to be done, as Ireland has the smallest proportion of evangelicals in the English-speaking world.

France has the third largest population in wider Europe, and the country is one of the most influential. The French are proud of their intellectual achievements and cultural standards. The French Revolution of 1789–93 had a dramatic effect and today France rigidly separates church and state: it allows freedom of religion, but prevents religion from permeating civic life in any way. In one sense, its religion is secularism, as can be seen when, after death, an important national figure is admitted to the Pantheon. Although three quarters of French people claim to be Roman Catholics, only about 10% of them attend church regularly, or even own a Bible, and only 20% are baptised into Catholicism as infants. The many religious conflicts throughout history, and the close link between the Catholic Church and the *ancien régime*, have made French people generally cynical about organized religion. A quarter of the population declares itself as having no religion.

Protestantism in France is weaker than it used to be. During the Reformation almost half the population were Protestant, leading to civil war between Catholics and Protestants, led by different noble groups. On 22 August 1572, 3,000 Protestants were killed in Paris in the St Bartholomew's Day massacre.

---

4. Though as we write, progressive politicians have had significant failure in two referenda on aspects of the progressive social agenda.

Religious toleration was established in 1589, but the conversion to Catholicism of the Protestant victor, Henry of Navarre in 1598 led to gradually increasing pressure on the Protestant Huguenots, and eventually in 1685 the revocation of the Edict of Nantes (which made it illegal to be a Protestant in France) and the flight of 400,000 Huguenots to Protestant countries, to the considerable commercial and military benefit of those countries and detriment to France. Most French Protestants today are in the northeast and the southeast of France; many of these are only nominal Christians.

Huge areas of French society are virtually untouched by the gospel and many French people will never come across a committed Christian in their lifetime. 50 million out of 64 million French people have no real link with a Christian church. Of the 37,000 communes, around 35,000 of them have no evangelical or pentecostal church. More than 300 towns with populations in excess of 10,000 people have no evangelical presence. France also has the third largest Jewish community in the world and as well as a large Muslim community. Surprisingly, the occult is also popular in France. Missionary work in France is made difficult by the fact that the French see themselves as Europe's cultural leaders, who have little to learn from those from outside their culture. Evangelicals are frequently regarded as a religious 'sect'.

Despite the challenges, there are also encouragements. Evangelical Christianity has been growing steadily for the past eighty years. There are high levels of commitment among them, and they are younger on average than the population as a whole. In 1940, the total number of Protestants in France was only 40,000. By 1980, evangelicals alone numbered 27,000, and today they exceed 600,000, as result in particular of Pentecostal penetration and immigration of committed Christians from Africa. These numbers are still small compared to the overall population, but going in the right direction.

The Netherlands, Germany, Austria, Belgium and Switzerland (which is not a member state of the EU) share history and culture. Apart from Belgium (until the Napoleonic wars, the Austrian Netherlands), these countries were the heartland of the Reformation, and the first European nations to send out Protestant missionaries to the non-Christian world. They were also nations which experienced a huge transformation as a result of the two World Wars which caused destruction and suffering. Consequently, after 1945 these nations became more preoccupied with building their wealth again than with taking Christianity to the rest of the world, though the Brethren and Pentecostals from these countries have been remarkably missionary-minded. Moreover, from the Enlightenment onwards, the German-speaking world became a fertile ground for liberal theologians who questioned and criticized the Bible, and divested it of its supernatural content.

While these nations recovered economically after the wars, Germany was divided by the Cold War, with its eastern half becoming known, somewhat ironically, as the German Democratic Republic. The famous Berlin Wall divided many families for decades, until the collapse of communism in eastern Europe and German reunification.

Reunified **Germany** is the largest country in the mid-west and an economic powerhouse. It accounts for one third of the industrial output of the EU and is the fourth largest economy in the world. Religiously Germany has been divided since the Reformation. Following the Reformation era, Catholic and Protestant princes fought against each other and later the many different states of Germany were ruled either by the Catholic Habsburgs and their clients or Protestant Prussians and others.

Germany was the centre of nineteenth-century liberal theology, the impact of which has continued to affect German churches. Many official Protestant Churches in Germany are liberal and this has contributed to the overall decline of Christian commitment, which is particularly marked in the former East Germany where 80% of the population are unchurched and 65% are agnostic or atheist (a statistic that may be the product of forty-five years of communist indoctrination in East Germany as much as liberal theology).

There are, however, large fellowship groups throughout Germany led by ministers who have neither state recognition nor theological degrees, but have effective ministries. In addition, there are Free Churches which reflect both Charismatic and non-Charismatic spirituality and many are evangelical, though they represent only 2.1% of the population. Between 1988 and 1995, over 1,000 Free Churches were planted. But despite all this activity, church attendance in Germany continues to fall.

Switzerland has a unique political system and such a commitment to neutrality that it is not even a member of the United Nations. Like Germany, it is religiously divided between Catholics and Protestants, though the dominance of either group varies, depending on the canton (until 1798, cantons were either one or the other). There is, however, a decline in both traditions, with church rolls being halved over the past 30 years. Lack of clergy in the Catholic Church, and liberalism among Protestants, have been contributary factors. There are encouraging signs among evangelical and Pentecostal denominations,[5] but they face an uphill task in this wealthy nation, in which the government survey of 2020 indicated that 31% of citizens were of no religion.

The **Netherlands** also has a Protestant and Catholic mix, with Protestants tending to live in the north and Catholics in the south of the country. Over half the population have no link with church, and a quarter classify themselves as non-religious. The nation as a whole is one of the most decadent and liberated on earth. The Netherlands was the first country to legalise euthanasia and is a world leader in New Age beliefs. In reality, the Netherlands is more known for its permissiveness than for its significant Christian past. Less than 10% of the population attend church weekly. Despite this, overall numbers of active Christians are increasing and the Charismatic renewal movement has had a significant impact. There is also a strong infrastructure of Christian publishing, broadcasting, theological education, and an increasing interest in mission.

Austria and Belgium are both Roman Catholic countries, but this does not tell the full story. **Austria** has seen a significant decline both in church attendance and of those ordained into the priesthood, even though the majority of Austrians believe in God. In the 1990s, the membership loss from the Catholic Church was 40,000 a year, and this trend continues. Most people have no real connection with the church, and a significant number of people have some dealings with the occult. Cults have also had an impact: the Jehovah's Witnesses are the third largest denomination after the Catholic and Lutheran churches. Evangelicals are a tiny minority, and, since 1998, formal recognition for smaller religious groups (including evangelicals) has been made more difficult. In 1985, there were 55 towns with populations in excess of 5,000 that had no evangelical witness, and this situation has not improved much. Most evangelical churches struggle to find pastors, and there is a need

---

5. The proportion of Christians who are neither Catholic nor state Protestants (Calvinists) has grown from less than 1% in 1960 to 5.6% in both 2010 and 2020.

for a new generation of trained leaders. Young people are often more open to the gospel, however, and there is an effective ministry among students.

Belgium has also seen dwindling support for the Catholic Church and only around 7% attend Mass. The priesthood is ageing and dwindling. Meanwhile, the cults, the occult and neo-pagans have attracted a great deal of attention. The country is deeply divided between the Walloons in the south and east and the Flemish in the north and west, and this affects economics, politics, and religious life. Evangelicals are experiencing slow growth and are hampered by a lack of Christian workers and pastors: only 40% of Flemish-speaking congregations having an indigenous pastor. Despite these challenges, some evangelical denominations are planting churches, and this offers hope to what is one of the most spiritually needy countries in Europe. Brussels is a key city with a population of over 1 million, of which 32% are non-Belgians and 13% Muslim.

Lying to the east of Germany is **Czechia** (and Slovakia (see below) which, together with the Czech lands, from 1919 formed Czechoslovakia, until Slovakia became independent in 1993). They were freed from communism in a bloodless revolution and since then Czechia has successfully transformed itself into a market economy, but this has been accompanied by a variety of social problems. From a spiritual perspective, the needs are great with 70% of the population considering themselves to be non-religious and the Catholic church declining rapidly. Evangelicals are few in number, and have much to do to win their fellow countrymen. Protestants (including evangelicals) in Czechia are experiencing freedom from persecution for only the second time since 1620. Protestantism has played an important role in the country's history, and today some lives are being changed as a result of Charismatic renewal. There is a considerable shortage of trained leadership, and many young people are leaving to work elsewhere.

Luxembourg is a small enclave which provides a base for several EU institutions and almost half the population are expatriates. Though traditionally the country is Catholic, most people in Luxembourg do not practise their faith, and secularism, as well as Eastern mysticism, play an important role in society. The Jehovah's Witnesses have made greater inroads than any evangelical group. Many of Luxembourg's evangelicals are foreigners.

Lichtenstein is a tiny Catholic constitutional principality linked to Switzerland. Most people do not practise their faith. The numbers of Muslims and non-religious people are growing, and there is only one evangelical fellowship started by British, Norwegian and Swiss believers.

Monaco is equally tiny and is a constitutional monarchy which is a home for the rich and famous. The population that is 75% expatriate. It is traditionally Catholic. There are only a few evangelicals, whose influence is small.

COUNTRY	POPULATION	% EVANGELICALS
Austria	9,106,126	0.5
Belgium	11,665,930	1.2
Czechia	10,526,937	0.7
France	68,042,591	1
Germany	84,270,625	2.1
Ireland	5,123,536	1.5
Lichtenstein	39,327	0.5
Luxembourg	647,599	0.5
Monaco	36,469	1.2
Netherlands	17,858,790	4.3
Switzerland	8,740,472	4.4
United Kingdom	67,026,292	8.8

The Sunshine States

Along the shores of the Mediterranean lie the sun-kissed lands of Europe. These are popular holiday destinations for northern Europeans, but they also present spiritual challenges.

Italy was the centre of the Roman Empire. The legacy was enormous: Roman law, the Latin language, culture and innovation, and this was added to by medieval Catholic thought and the Renaissance. From the fifth to the mid-nineteenth centuries, Italy was a loose connection of independent territories and city states. The country was unified in 1861, at first as a constitutional monarchy. During World War 1, the Italians fought with the Allies against the Germans, but under Mussolini fought with the Nazis during World War 2 until Italy's surrender in 1943.

Italy became a republican democracy in 1946, and for its first decades looked likely to elect a substantial Communist Party to government. While governments were short-lived—averaging one every 12 months since 1946, for many years they were mainly Christian Democratic in character and thereby linked to Catholic social thought; and the leading figures in government became familiar from year to year. One of the most constant features of Italian society has been organised crime, with networks such as the Sicilian Mafia, Neapolitan Camorra and now the Calabrian 'Ndrangheta exerting significant power. Successive governments and the judiciary have tried to stamp it out, but with limited success. Though the Catholic Church ceased to be the established state religion in 1984, it is still dominant in the national psyche, though it is estimated that more than 10 million people have left the church in recent decades. The occult and cults are growing rapidly. Evangelicals are more numerous in the poorer south than they are in the prosperous north. On the whole, they are weak and scattered, but there are encouraging signs of increased collaboration across denominations. The need for expatriate workers to help the Italian church is as great as ever, but for many years there has been a high attrition rate.

Spain is a country with a remarkable history and diversity. Since the expulsion of the Islamic Moors at the end of the fifteenth century, Spain has been strongly Roman Catholic. It established a widespread empire in south and central America in the sixteenth century, and the wealth drawn from there made it a great power in Europe until well into the eighteenth century. Following the Napoleonic Wars, Spain struggled for 150 years to establish stable constitutional government and democracy. Three years of civil war ended in 1939 with a right-wing dictatorship which lasted 35 years and which was closely linked to the Catholic Church. The civil war, followed by World War 2, disrupted missionary input, though, by keeping a low profile, mission workers were increasingly able to return from 1945 onwards. By the 1960s, tourism (of increasing importance to the country) was beginning to open it up to northern European influence. Spain's somewhat fragile liberal democracy that succeeded Franco has opened the country to the full force of the political and social trends that western Europe has been experiencing since the 1960s.

Most Spaniards identify themselves as Catholics and only 4% say that they are non-religious. Only 15% of the population, however, attend church (though this is one of the higher proportions in Europe). It would not be an understatement to suggest that the Catholic Church in Spain is in crisis. Few are applying for the priesthood and rapid changes in social attitudes in recent decades have eroded moral foundations. Secularisation has increased to the point at whichSpanish young people are among the most spiritually disengaged in Europe. Drugs and gambling are major problems.

With the rapid rise in secularism, conflict has arisen between secularizers and traditional Catholics who tend to be conservative. Although complete religious freedom was granted in 1978, there is still a great deal of prejudice against Protestants. Evangelicals are also sometimes mistaken for Jehovah's Witnesses, who are the largest non-Catholic grouping.

The growth of Spanish Evangelicals is encouraging, though slow. Evangelicals need to come out from under the shadow of their despised minority status and use their religious freedom to the full. There are many under-reached areas, including 345 cities and towns with populations of over 5,000 that do not have an evangelical church. Of the new churches recently started, a significant proportion have been planted by Latinos from Latin America, who are now numerous in Spain.

Portugal is Spain's immediate neighbour and, though originally part of Spain, it gained independence in the twelfth century and became one of the major colonizing powers. In 1910, Portugal became a republic, but suffered a military coup in 1926. From then until 1968, it was ruled in a dictatorial manner by Prime Minister Salazar. A coup in 1974 brought about a coalition government and the restoration of democracy, after which the Portuguese colonies of Mozambique, Angola, Guinea-Bissau, Sao Tomé and Principe, and Cape Verde were granted independence.

Only after 1974 was religious freedom granted in Portugal, though the Roman Catholic Church still retains some privileges. Groups like the Jehovah's Witnesses and Mormons have seen dramatic growth since then, but many evangelical groups have not done so well. They have suffered division, as well as struggling with the dominance of Catholicism. Evangelicals are still regarded by many in Portugal as a sect, and the situation has been further complicated in recent years by Portugal's economic development, which owes much to its membership of the EU. The country is now more materialistic and less interested in spiritual matters. The Catholic Church has also lost some of its grip, particularly in central and southern Portugal where only around 3% attend Mass.

The future looks challenging for Portuguese evangelicals, not least because they have to handle the divisions caused by prosperity teaching among other things. There is also a need to rise to the challenge of mission. The Evangelical Alliance has a role to play here, and the widespread use of Portuguese in the world offers strategic opportunities, but there is a lack of trained leadership and full-time workers. In spite of these problems, there are still signs of growth among Portuguese evangelicals, especially among the Pentecostals and Charismatics.

The small island of **Malta** was the first European population to embrace Christianity after the Apostle Paul was shipwrecked there. Church attendance is high in this Catholic-dominated country and over 80% say that religion is important to them. But while Malta remains the most religious country in Europe, few people have any kind of personal walk with Christ. Catholic Charismatic groups are widespread in Malta, and the Alpha course is very popular among them. Until independence in 1964, there was little evangelical or Protestant witness among the people. Since then, there has been slow but steady growth. Not only does Malta need the gospel, but it is also a strategic meeting place for the many Libyans and Tunisians who travel through Malta.

The tiny Catholic enclave of **Andorra** is now a shopping destination for well-heeled tourists. Priests hold little sway in the country, and many people would rather consult mediums and astrologers. The handful of evangelical churches are in a difficult position.

San Marino, which has ties with Italy, has been an independent republic since AD 301. While it is a Catholic city, few practise their faith and the pressure exerted on Evangelicals means that no churches or ministries currently evangelise there. The church barely even exists.

Vatican City, which is officially a state in its own right, exerts a significant influence on Catholics around the world, and the Pope remains one of the world's most influential persons. The Catholic Church faces many challenges today and the 120 million strong Catholic charismatic movement has brought a significant amount of renewal and energy.

COUNTRY	POPULATION	% EVANGELICAL
Andorra	79,824	0.4
Italy	58,883,079	1.1
Malta	533,286	1.3
Portugal	10,270,865	3
San Marino	33,661	0
Spain	47,558,630	1
Vatican City	519	2

The Levant and Caucasus

We refer here to a few countries in western Asia which can be seen as part of wider Europe, either for historical reasons or because, in one case, it is recognised as a candidate to join the European Union.

Turkey is unusual amongst European nations in that it crosses two continents, part of Turkey being in Europe (including the great city of Istanbul with its population of nearly 17 million) and part in Asia (Anatolia). Even though many Turks do not consider themselves to be European, Turkey has nevertheless been seeking EU membership for many years, and inclusion remains a possibility.[6] That said, the government seems to be increasingly dictatorial and anti-European, which has caused concern among EU member states.

Officially, Turkey has been secular since the days of Kemal Ataturk in the 1920s, but it is overwhelmingly Muslim with a small Christian population. During the Ottoman Empire, Turkey was guardian of Islam's holy places and its chief protagonist. Today, the Orthodox Church has a modest presence in a region which it dominated for centuries. Evangelical Christianity is very small, but growing. As recently as 1960, there were only a dozen evangelicals in the country, but, by the year 2000, there were 34 fellowships with a membership of about 2,000; by 2003, there were 3,000 evangelicals meeting in 76 fellowships. These numbers continue to rise. Most of Turkey's 81 provinces

---

6. This remains one of the most hotly disputed political issues in Turkey.

have Christian believers, but many do not have churches. Some Muslims have becoming increasingly radicalised, and there is an ongoing hostility towards Christianity. Legally, Turkey allows freedom of religion, but in practice this does not amount to very much, and Christians find it very difficult to witness in that environment.

No missionaries as such are allowed in Turkey, though many have supported themselves by other employment. However, the task is monumental. One important focal point is literature. Istanbul has a much-visited Christian bookshop run by the Bible Society and there are also several Turkish Christian publishing houses which produce Bibles and a limited number of Christian book titles.

Cyprus became a divided country in 1974, due to the Turkish invasion and occupation of the north-eastern part of the island, which resulted in population transfer in both directions between the two parts of the island. The north is the Turkish Republic of Northern Cyprus, and the south, the Republic of Cyprus which is Greek-speaking and, with wide international support, still lays claim to the whole island. The partition has caused deep and bitter divisions with little sign of any kind of resolution. The Republic of Cyprus has fared better economically than its northern counterpart which relies heavily on Turkish subsidies. Spiritually, both parts are needy. The Orthodox Church provides a sense of national identity for Greek Cypriots and, while Cyprus is religious by European standards and church attendance is high, that is more evident among older people and people in rural areas. Evangelicals number only a few, even though Cyprus is an important base for Christian organisations working in the Levant and Near East. There are vibrant churches in the ethnic minority communities, such as English-speaking people and Filipinos. These need to reach out to the indigenous population.

Israel and **Lebanon** are situated in western Asia, but both have strong European links. Israel has experienced an increased interest in the gospel in recent years, especially among Jews, now with more than 12,000 Jews recognising Jesus as Messiah. Given the wider political and religious tensions, it is perhaps unsurprising that the Christian church in Israel is fragmented, though some signs of unity are evident.

Lebanon has had decades of war and unrest, deriving from divisions between its Christian and Muslim populations. Insecurity has displaced around 80% of the population, and many have emigrated, particularly to north America. The country has been traumatised by this and, as a consequence, the Christian population has fallen from 62% in 1970 to under 32% today. Orthodox and Catholic churches have struggled for survival in the midst of traditionalism, but there have been some revival movements. Meanwhile, Protestant churches have struggled to be accepted.

COUNTRY	POPULATION	% EVANGELICAL
Cyprus	1,251,489	0.8
Israel	9,038,309	0.4
Lebanon	5,489,740	0.5
Turkey	85,816,199	0

Central and Eastern Europe

We now come to the part of Europe that once lay behind the so-called 'iron curtain' and has only recently opened up to mission activity.

We begin with **Poland** which became a governmental entity in the eleventh century, but its history has been one of occupation and hardship. Most recently, during World War 2, one quarter of the population lost their lives. This was followed by a period of communism which was reversed by the Solidarity protests, resulting in the formation of a multi-party democracy in 1989.

Since the fall of communism, Poland has prospered. It became a member of NATO in 1999 and joined the EU in 2004. With its programme of economic reform, Poland has transformed itself into one of the most robust economies in central Europe, as well as one of the strongest militarily. Spiritually, however, Poland remains a needy place. There is freedom of religion, but the Catholic Church is strong and influential, and for many Poles is integral to their sense of national identity. It is also conservative and has a strong theological commitment to the veneration of Mary and the saints. However, there may be signs that some Poles have less need of Catholicism, given their newfound prosperity.

Evangelicals are only a tiny minority in Poland; they suffer low-level discrimination; and are often seen as a sect. This confusion is compounded by the fact that the Jehovah's Witnesses are very active in Poland and outnumber evangelicals, who are often divided. The formation of an Evangelical Alliance in 1999 has brought hope of unity, and some church planting is also taking place. As Polish young people are eager to learn, teaching English is one of the great opportunities for bridge-building.

Slovakia also has a strong Christian heritage, but Catholic, Lutheran and Reformed churches are all struggling with low attendance, though there are some renewal movements, especially among Lutherans. The few evangelical denominations that exist are small, but there is a desire to reach out and even to church plant. This task is formidable, as there are many towns with little by way of evangelical witness. There is a significant challenge from the Jehovah's Witnesses, who are more numerous that all evangelicals put together. Slovakia has significant minority groups such as Hungarians and Gypsies, and these have proved challenging to reach.

Further to the south are **Hungary** and Romania. Prior to 1918, the Austro-Hungarian Empire was one of the great European powers. It then broke up, so that Hungary today occupyies only 40% of its former territory. In the closing stages of WW2, Hungary was occupied by the Soviet Union and it was agreed that it should continue within the sphere of influence of the Soviets. This put communists in Hungary in the position to convert the country into a one-party state, which was achieved in 1949, and that ended only in 1989. This period saw a great deal of tragedy, not least during the 1956 uprising when 80,000 Hungarians were killed and a further 200,000 fled to the West. Since becoming a multi-party democracy, Hungary has joined NATO (1999) and the EU (2003). It has also developed economically and has enjoyed an increased standard of living.

Christianity arrived in Hungary 1,000 years ago and today there is freedom of religion, though smaller evangelical groups have had to fight for equal treatment under changes introduced by Victor Orban. The majority of the population are Catholic, but alongside a sizable Protestant minority. There are also lots of spiritual alternatives, including the occult, eastern mysticism, pagan witchcraft, Magyar shamanism, and Buddhism. Evangelicals are relatively few in number and lack of commitment is often a challenge. However, most Hungarian towns have an evangelical church, however small. Some parts of

the country are more spiritually alive than others, but there remains a great
need for evangelism in the country as a whole. Hungary's Gypsy community
is significant and one that experiences economic disadvantage. It is less evangelised than Gypsy communities in neighbouring countries. There are also signs
of spiritual hunger, despite resistance to the gospel in much of the country.
Hungary is also a central European hub for theological education, as well as
being strategically located, surrounded as it is by seven adjacent countries.

Romania suffered under communism and still lags behind some of its
former iron curtain neighbours. From a spiritual point of view, however,
Romania fares better than most. The Orthodox Church accounts for 87% of
the population and, while there is more religious freedom now than under
communism, the Orthodox Church opposes religious minorities, including
evangelicals. Within the Orthodox Church, there is a renewal movement
known as the Lord's Army, which numbers some 300,000 and has close links
with the Romanian Evangelical Alliance. Evangelicals in Romania have not
always been united, but there is growth and around 100 new churches are
planted every year. In Romania, Gypsies are a despised minority who suffer
discrimination and lack economic opportunity. They are spiritually responsive,
and evangelism in this community has been helped by the completion of the
Bible in Kalderash. There are also significant spiritual needs in the southeast,
where there are far fewer churches. Christians in Romania have a strong interest
in cross-cultural mission and Romanian missionaries can more easily access
some mission fields than Western missionaries.

Belarus gained independence from the USSR in August 1991, but still
operates as a communist-era authoritarian regime. While preferential treatment
is given to Orthodox and Catholic churches and there is state hostility towards
evangelicals, the latter are nevertheless growing. The work is difficult, however,
as house churches are banned, as is ministering outside your home city or using
literature that has not been approved by the state. All religious activity must
also have state approval and obtaining property for a church to rent or buy
is a huge problem. There is also the danger that the indigenous church will
become isolated as foreign missionary presence is slowly being squeezed out.

Ukraine is a significant gateway between East and West, which makes
it vulnerable. It has a strong Christian legacy and, while evangelicals have

historically faced persecution, they have emerged all the stronger for it. Freedom of religion has improved, but it is not yet a legal right. Tension has also existed between Orthodox, Catholics and Protestants. New churches have emerged and brought a renewed vision for evangelism and growth. This, however, is being hampered by the war which is causing enormous material damage to the country. Only time will tell what the long-term consequences will be.

Moldova is the poorest country in Europe and, given its systemic problems, that is unlikely to change in the near future. The area of Transnistria functions as a separate state with support from Russia, and organised crime, human trafficking and alcohol and drug abuse are considerable problems. The Orthodox Church makes life difficult for evangelicals, who are nevertheless growing in number. One significant challenge is that poverty has forced many pastors and Christians to leave the country.

The Baltic states of **Lithuania**, **Latvia** and **Estonia** have all grown economically since the fall of the Soviet Union, but their newfound freedoms have also led to materialism and an increase in moral and social problems. Of the three, Latvia has the highest proportion of evangelicals and the moral climate seems to have galvanised and united Christians. Mission vision, while in its infancy in the country, is nevertheless present and there is a growing desire to reach out and plant churches. Religious freedom in Estonia opened the door to both evangelical ministries and cults, including pagan religions. Most of the population needs to be re-evangelised. In Lithuania, the Catholic Church maintains significant influence, and there is evidence of new growth among charismatic Catholics. The Lutheran, Reformed and Orthodox churches are all struggling, and many of the established evangelical denominations are tradition bound and lack vibrancy. There is, however, some exciting growth among new churches.

COUNTRY	POPULATION	% EVANGELICAL
Belarus	9,534,955	1.3
Estonia	1,326,062	4.9
Hungary	9,678,000	2.8
Latvia	1,850,651	7.0

Lithuania	2,750,055	1.1
Moldova	3,272,996	3.7
Poland	37,749,000	0.3
Romania	19,053,815	5.4
Slovakia	5,428,792	1.2
Ukraine	39,701,739	3.8

The Balkans and Greece

Greece became independent from the Ottoman Empire in 1827, after 400 years of Ottoman rule. Tensions with the successor, Turkey, still exist following the Greco-Turkish War of 1919–22, when Greece sought to occupy much of north and west Anatolia, and Greece has also been troubled with two civil wars and two dictatorships in the past fifty years. Today, Greece is a republic and a parliamentary democracy. Like Turkey, it is a member of NATO, but unlike its neighbour it already has EU membership which has brought stability, modernisation and commerce. Greece has the largest shipping fleet in the EU and a growing tourist industry.

In religion, Greece is predominantly Orthodox, with a measure of religious freedom, though the small evangelical community, which numbers only about 15,000, faces some discrimination. During the centuries of Ottoman rule, the Orthodox Church was a focal point for Greek identity and still all other religious groups are treated with suspicion. To leave the Orthodox Church is to become less Greek and therefore a dilution of the Greek way of life. This makes evangelistic work very difficult. There are some true believers within the Orthodox Church, but they are few and far between.

Among the most spiritually needy in Greece are the immigrants and the island communities. There are approximately 150 Greek islands that have no resident Christian witness. Literature work has proved successful in Greece and there are many Greeks who live abroad (in USA 2 million, Germany 500,000 and Australia 272,000). Within these communities, there are evangelical churches and this could provide a source of missionaries to reach their spiritually impoverished homeland. There is great need for sustained evangelism and discipleship.

During communism, Yugoslavia was one country, but after the death of Tito (1980) and the collapse of communism in 1990, it fragmented into six separate republics. This was followed by the devastating Balkan wars which precipitated UN and NATO involvement, and added two further independent states (Montenegro and Kosovo). This is the most ethnically diverse part of Europe and the conflict has served to entrench existing prejudices.

Slovenia has developed the most economically, due to its trading links with central and western Europe, since 2004 as a member of the European Union. It has a strong Catholic tradition, but little spiritual vitality. Nominalism is on the increase and atheism is widespread. Evangelicals are a tiny minority and lack trained leadership. One bright ray of hope is the new translation of the Bible. Some Christian groups worked together to ensure its widespread distribution through schools and secular bookshops. Christian resources are in short supply, so there is a need for the production of quality materials. There is also a great need for church planting and outreach ministries.

Bosnia and Herzegovina was Europe's second poorest country before the Balkan war. The war shattered its agrarian economy and now foreign aid is a key source of income. Culturally, Bosnia straddles East and West. During the 500-year Ottoman occupation, most Bosnians became Muslim. The Serb, Croat, Bosnian war caused immense damage to Bosnia and the country suffered partition. Today, there is an uneasy peace with deep divisions along ethnic lines. Theoretically, there is religious freedom. However, the scars run deep and consequently this is not so in practice. Life is a real struggle for evangelicals, though there is growth. In 1991, there were three congregations and now there are about 35. The church in Bosnia greatly needs outside help.

Croatia and Serbia were bitter rivals within Yugoslavia between 1919 and 1990. During the Balkan war in the 1990s, Croatia lost a lot of its territory to Serbia, but regained it again through diplomacy. Hatred of Serbs and Bosnians is still a prominent feature of national life in Croatia. With the link between ethnicity and religion in the region, Croats have become spiritually resistant, due to their commitment to Catholicism. However, Evangelicals have been able to relate to all the ethnic groups, and this has produced results. There is need for church planting, but what growth there is has been encouraging. Croatia and the whole region has been greatly helped by the Evangelical Theological Seminary in Osijek, which is producing Christian workers.

Since its defeat by the Turks in 1389, **Serbia** has rarely been an independent nation. It was ruled by the Ottomans and, then, partly by the Austrio-Hungarian empire with the southern part as an independent principality from 1817. This history developed a strong nationalism and when Yugoslavia began to unravel, Serbia found itself in the centre of the Balkan conflict.

The Serbian Orthodox church is strong and is an avenue for expressing nationalism. Serbians also see themselves as a European bulwark against the encroachment of Islam. Consequently, Christian mission organisations find it hard to get established in Serbia.

Evangelicals are a tiny minority and face significant pressure. There is a lack of unity among evangelicals though the Evangelical Alliance has a role to play. In addition, there is a lack of trained leaders. The KES Bible School which is interdenominational, but has links with the Brethren and Baptists, is small, needs funding, has a limited curriculum, and relies heavily on foreign input.

Montenegro shares Orthodox Christianity with Serbia, but little else. Many Montenegrins are embarrassed by their former association with Serbia (which was ended in a referendum in Montenegro in 2006) and are fiercely independent. In both nations, democracy is fragile, and the growing strength of the Serbian Orthodox Church could cause problems, not least in the realm of religious freedom.

People in Montenegro remain deeply divided as to their relationship with Serbia, and the situation remains volatile as a result. The Montenegrin Orthodox church has worked hard to establish itself in place of the Serbian Orthodox church, but spiritual nominalism is an issue. The evangelical church is tiny, but there is some growth. This mountainous enclave is one of the most spiritually needy places on earth.

Kosovo has a small but growing evangelical community. There were around 80 believers when the war broke out in 1998 and now there are over 2,000 and around 35 evangelical churches. Kosovo declared independence from Serbia in 2008 and, while this is recognised by many nations, Serbia is unlikely to allow full independence. Meanwhile, ethnic rivalries run deep in the country. Most Kosovan Albanians are Muslims and radicalism is on the rise, often encouraged through funding from the Middle East. While mosques get built, Christian churches get damaged and destroyed by angry mobs. This is a needy country in a precarious situation.

North Macedonia is another part of the jigsaw that is the Balkans, and one of the poorest. The dominant feature of the political and social fabric of this nation is its ethnic diversity with ethnic Albanians feeling a closer connection to Albania and Kosovo than to their fellow countrymen. They make up one third of the population; are mainly, if not almost completely, Muslim; are growing in number due to a higher birth-rate; and are demanding more rights. The Orthodox Church, though weak, is the dominant religious grouping, though its approximately 1,000 churches are largely empty, as Macedonians are generally secular in their thinking. Evangelicals are a tiny minority with less than 100 congregations, but they are growing. There is also a sizable Romani minority community, which is poor and oppressed, and practises a mixture of Islam and folk superstition.

Albania, like Bosnia, has a large Muslim population and its location in the Balkans has meant that it has been adversely affected by the troubles of its neighbours. It remains an unstable country, struggling to get to grips with democracy. Evangelical Christians are a small but growing minority and, given how closed Albania was under the tyranny of Enver Hoxha, it is amazing to see what growth has taken place. There are now over 160 churches in Albania linked with the Evangelical Alliance, and there are also indigenous leaders and national networks. There is a long road ahead, and a great need for leadership training. Many Albanian towns and villages have no evangelical witness. Leadership training is a key issue, as is mission vision. It can be argued that Albania is the best-placed nation to reach into Montenegro, Kosovo, and North Macedonia.

Bulgaria suffered under communism, and continues to suffer today with corruption, poverty and crime networks prominent, notwithstanding membership of the European Union since 2007. The Orthodox Church was divided during communism, due to the collusion of Orthodox leaders with the communist regime. It is badly in need of renewal. There are 2,500 villages with no evangelical witness, and a need for more churches in the cities. Leadership training is also a key need, as heresy and the cults cause damage to the spiritual life of this country.

COUNTRY	POPULATION	% EVANGELICAL
Greece	10,432,481	0.4
Bulgaria	6,781,953	1.9
Albania	2,793,592	0.5
Bosnia & Herzegovina	3,320,954	0.1
Croatia	3,871,833	0.4
Kosovo	1,659,714	0.1
Montenegro	617,683	0.1
North Macedonia	1,832,696	0.2
Serbia	6,647,003	0.6
Slovenia	2,119,844	0.1

This is the Europe of today—a highly diverse region where there are deep spiritual needs almost everywhere. It is one of the great mission priorities of our day and one to which the church must commit itself, as we obey the demands of the Great Commission. There are many places in the world where evangelism is easier with more results. The changes in central and eastern Europe, and the Balkans, brought about the collapse of the Soviet Union in 1989–91 opened doors of gospel opportunity. For the most part, those doors remain open. But in most of these places, we have scarcely begun to scratch the surface of what is possible. We must not allow the resurgence of local nationalisms in Europe to prevent the church (the forerunner of a universal Kingdom, which the kings of the earth will acknowledge by bringing their tribute into it) from responding to the spiritual needs that continue there. Nor, in the west of Europe, can we allow the tremendous gospel work of centuries, certainly since the Reformation, simply to be expunged as if it had never been. Surely, we must fight the spiritual battle for these areas.

In the next chapter we will investigate this further, looking at the unique challenge that reaching Europe for Christ will be.

Chapter 6

Twenty-first century Europe—
the mission imperative

A s we think about the data and analysis already presented in this volume, it is important to contrast Europe (and the European sphere, for much of what has been described also affects Canada, Australia and New Zealand, though less so the United States) with many other places in the world in terms of the fortunes of biblical Christianity. In Europe, the position has changed radically since the year 1750.

European exceptionalism—the shift of global Christianity southwards

Until the year 1500, Christianity was largely confined to Europe and the Near East, and there was only hazy knowledge of other parts of the world. Between 1500 and 1750, that was changed by the expansion of the Spanish and Portuguese empires in Latin America and South and East Asia (though in the latter area, it was a question of trading enclaves rather than wholesale occupation as in what we now call Latin America). Unsurprisingly, given the entrenched position of the Catholic Church in Spain and Portugal, and its close relation with the Spanish and Portuguese crowns, it was virtually automatic that Catholic Christianity spread as their empires extended, though the courage, perseverance, and self-sacrifice of the Catholic missionary orders in the process should not be underestimated.

By contrast, Protestantism was comparatively slow in recognizing the call of the extra-European missionary task. That eventually followed from German Pietism and the evangelical revivalism that it spawned in the eighteenth century. Evangelicalism soon awakened to the missionary task and it quickly became a true flood. If anything, in the nineteenth century, evangelical mission tended to precede colonisation as countless missionaries took seriously the Pauline ambition of preaching the gospel where Christ had not yet already been named (see Romans 15: 20)—though evangelical mission also readily followed and took advantage of colonisation.

When the methods of evangelical mission are taken into account (largely depending on individual initiative and calling, without close central direction), the spread of evangelical Christianity in the nineteenth and twentieth centuries has been remarkable. This has been true in both Latin America where it was preceded by Catholicism and in sub-Saharan Africa where the religious environment was that of tribal animism. Consequently today, while there are some 18m evangelical Christians in Europe (2.5% of the total population), there are some 545m worldwide and 272m in Africa and Latin America.[1] It is remarkable that European evangelicalism is so influential in the world even though only 1 in 30 of the world's evangelical Christians are Europeans. Moreover, numbers are static or reducing in Europe, but still growing in the rest of the world. In Europe, there is the risk that evangelical Christianity will be sidelined in its historic heartlands in the British Isles, Scandinavia and northern Germany. The mission task is unfinished in France, the Iberian Peninsula and Italy. It has scarcely begun in most of eastern Europe and certainly in the Balkans and Greece, even though it was started well over 100 years ago. Here are fields in need of labourers (Mt. 9: 36–38), and there is room for plenty of them.

Implications: does Europe matter still as a harvest field?

This has implications for mission strategy. Of course, there is something in the managerial argument that it is more sensible to reinforce success (that is, put our efforts into the Majority World) than failure (in Europe). But that raises the question whether this argument represents a Kingdom or worldly strategy, and whether, in many parts of the Majority World, evangelical Christianity is strong enough for growth to be a local responsibility, leaving transnational mission resources to be focused on areas of gospel need or which have not yet

---

1. These figures are from the 2010 edition of *Operation World*. They may be greater today, especially if evangelical, Pentecostal, and Charismatic Christians were counted together.

begun to be reached in any practical way. It is certainly ironic, and possibly questionable, that mission service groups and mission-orientated churches in the West are still sending significant numbers of cross-cultural missionaries to parts of the world, like sub-Saharan Africa, where the church is thriving and growing strongly. Of course, areas like sub-Saharan Africa do need specialists who offer things not yet available within those countries, such as theological educators and medical specialists. These missionaries will help to develop and mature the church there. But to be truly strategic, we must ask where the need is globally. Moreover, missionaries require funding and, in sheer financial terms, it often costs much less to support and equip indigenous workers in these countries, if such workers can be found. The relative size and health of the church in places like sub-Saharan Africa needs to be factored in to our thinking, especially when Europe, which has huge spiritual needs, lacks the mission personnel needed to do the job!

There is also the question of whether we are to regard Europe as already a lost cause, to be abandoned to its own rejection of faith and infidelity; or whether it is simply too soon to do that. Equally, there is a question of whether the reservoirs of Christian thought are still so present not only to the collective European mind, but to many individual European minds, that there remains a potentially fruitful ground for biblical evangelism, especially when approached through avenues of their thought that remain essentially Christian.

Whatever the answers to these questions, it remains the case that there is deep spiritual need in many places in Europe and maybe even spiritual hunger, if only we can engage effectively with those concerned. Certainly, many Europeans have renounced God—or are convinced that he is merely a remote, vague life-force, or spiritual principle, who is not really interested in the way that we live. There is also a sense with some that in the final analysis God will welcome us into heaven however we have lived our lives and whatever we have thought about him. (This is often coupled with the conviction that humans should simply immerse themselves in doing what comes naturally, and that God has little interest in how we live our lives.) All these ways of thinking are doing their damage in terms of, at the very least, human contentment, if not mental health and destructive patterns of thought and behaviour. And there is little inclination to count the costs imposed on our nearest and dearest of adhering to the principles of absolute individual freedom and individual autonomy.

These may simply be complicated ways of saying that Europe, north, east, west and south, constitutes a major mission need and a major mission opportunity. It would be tragic if ignorance or neglect were to lead us as Christian believers to miss the opportunity and calling to take the good news of the gospel in all its breadth and depth to our nearest neighbours in our European home. Mission in Europe may seem less glamourous to us, or even perhaps too easy and comfortable, compared with other possible mission locations. The re-evangelisation of the European heartlands, and the evangelisation of many parts of eastern Europe and the Balkans, are no mean objectives. But the challenge of the task should not be underestimated (as we shall consider in a moment).

For citizens of the UK, it would be particularly tragic if our withdrawal from the European Union (only one of the markers of European identity and only one particular European structure) were to lead us to turn our backs on continental Europe's right to and need for gospel. Should we allow that particular British political decision to over-ride our neighbours' need for the gospel? Should we deny them the gospel because they have the temerity to be Europeans, in respect of whom some of our newspapers at least are now rather contemptuous?

Challenges to mission to Europe

The call should not however obscure its challenges. Some are dealt with in detail elsewhere in this book. We call attention here to three generic questions which relate to how we engage effectively with today's Europeans in order to bring them to Christ and experience for themselves the transformation resulting from repentance, forgiveness and becoming new creatures in him.

Apologetics matter

The next chapter of this book considers in particular the difficulties about biblical Christianity that many Europeans will have, whatever their background and the particular national culture that they may inhabit. These difficulties need to be treated as real, not as manufactured, or a fake excuse, or evidence of sinfulness. It is important to treat people's intellectual difficulties and questions as honest doubts, which is what they will be in the great majority of cases, especially in view of the way that Europeans have been bombarded with religious scepticism from their earliest youth in education and through the media and even entertainment. If such Europeans are to receive the gospel, many will need to be shaken from their unbelief and their certainty that what they believe is right. (We should not underestimate the extent to which individual human beings believe that what they think is right and that that it is the only possible way to think.) An essential step in pre-evangelism with respect to such individuals is to cause them to wonder whether what they have apparently always thought is in fact correct. We ourselves shall need to be on top of the arguments on the key topics. Fortunately, people's main objections to the existence of God and the truth of Christianity are in essence limited in number, but we need to be able to engage effectively about them. Chapter 8 below and the related appendix are intended to help in the necessary preparation.

Manner and style in apologetics: friendly exploratory conversation between equals

But much more important than being on top of apologetic arguments is the *manner and style* in which we go about the discussion. (It is wise to avoid using the word 'apologetics' in their hearing or the people you are trying to engage with are likely to be extremely confused!) It must never become an argument or a dispute. It must not aim to convince (at least, certainly not in the immediate conversation), and certainly we should never appear to want to win the argument, still less to beat them into submission in intellectual debate. It is much better to be pursuing together a friendly exploratory conversation about ideas in which both parties are wanting not only to understand each other's arguments better, but to understand better the central points involved in the question. It is important to allow the person we are talking with to question our position, as well as vice versa, or it will become apparent that our only purpose is to demolish their position. In any case, the process of understanding our position will be likely to be illuminating for them. Friendly discussion of this kind is, with the help of the Holy Spirit, likely to throw light on the intellectual cracks in their position.

   It is important that they should not be told that they are wrong, but that they should come to their own conclusion that their position does not have the merits that they previously thought it had. Indeed, it is not essential as a first step towards conversion that they change their minds on all their previously held intellectual positions on Christianity. It will be sufficient for them to 'park' their intellectual reservations and be prepared to begin to explore biblical worldviews with us, not with respect to every detail of those worldviews of course, but on matters which are key to conversion and salvation, and above all to introduce them to Scripture which they are prepared to consider on at least neutral terms (as the work of the Holy Spirit, it has its own power to speak to the unbeliever unless their mind is completely closed to it).

Pitching the level of discussion

In such discussion, we need to pitch the level of conversation accurately to the needs of the person. In European culture today, particularly on the north and west of the landmass, given their socialisation and education, it is normal for people to have intellectual difficulties with Christianity without in any sense being intellectuals themselves—they may well have absorbed views, for example, from the popular music that they listen to, since for a couple of generations it has been fashionable for contemporary music to have a sceptical edge. These beliefs may be an obstacle to their considering the claims of Christianity. Our apologetics need to be pitched at the right level for the purpose.

To illustrate the point: the author of this chapter recalls in the mid-1960s a discussion with the lads of our church youth club. (We were a well-to-do church, with a youth club of lads of quite different background.) In the course of the discussion, one guy opined that he did not want to go to 'eaven, because he could not fink of anyfink more borin' than sit'in on a cold slab in a nightie playin' a 'arp for ever! There were several intellectual misconceptions in his brief statement, but the discussion needed to be pitched for someone who had left school at fifteen without qualifications. On the night, we probably did not manage it.

Informal friendship

Quite apart from apologetics, friendly exploratory conversations with people will begin to establish personal relationships with them. In today's Europe, people whether atheists, agnostics, or nominal non-practising Christians, are unlikely to become true Christians by going out of the blue to an evangelistic meeting or by attending church on a regular or irregular basis. Of course, that does occasionally happen: I became a Christian as a teenager in a purely secular meeting when my eyes were unexpectedly opened to the essence of the gospel, but I had the advantage of having been taken to church (as it happened, an evangelical church) from infancy and was catechized at a church school. But with rates of churchgoing being so low generally in Europe, particularly in western Europe, most people are going to need genuine friendship with a Christian believer or believers as an intermediate step towards understanding the basics of Christian faith and taking their own step to adopt it for themselves. This is not a high-productivity form of evangelism. (We should note that Pentecostals in their healing crusades are able to attract a certain segment of populations by those methods, particularly perhaps if that segment's access to healthcare is limited. What the British refer to as working-class communities, and certain minorities, evidently respond well to the Pentecostal style of evangelism through high-octane meetings including healing ministry. As many other evangelical groups are skewed more towards a middle-class constituency, mission workers from that background often struggle to connect with those whom Pentecostals find it easy to reach.)

Friendship evangelism is time-intensive on the part of believers: results are not always immediate and take significant investment of time with particular individuals, not always with success. This is why friendship evangelism has to be the work of the whole local Christian community—to be an every-member ministry: it cannot and must not be left only to professional missionaries, and especially not to expatriate ones.

Cultural assimilation

This highlights a wider point about expatriate missionary work in today's Europe. That is the need for immersion in and understanding not only of language, but of the *culture* in which the individual is working, bearing in mind the wide variation of national and regional cultures in Europe, and the importance to the individual European of his or her own local culture. It takes time, empathy, and willingness to learn the ways and idioms of a particular local culture and adapt to it. This goes further than head knowledge and anthropological study. Successfully to assimilate to a particular culture requires not only to learn to respect it, but in some sense also to 'love' it. If this can be shown, it will be noticed. On the contrary, if one remains essentially a critical observer (an outsider) whose sense of belonging to a different (and superior) culture is obvious to the local culture in which the expatriate is working, success will probably elude him or her. Spies or underground agents often give themselves away by being insufficiently assimilated to the culture in which they are operating: the challenge to the expatriate worker is similar. Here, it is a mistake to think that fluency in the language will be enough and that cultural fluency is an optional extra (though, of course, truly understanding a culture without fluency in its language is probably impossible): many an American mission worker has failed in Britain, for example, because they have assumed that, because the language is the same, the culture is the same.

Informality the watchword

This chapter has already begun to touch on this topic. For more than a thousand years, the Christian religion in Europe has been associated with formal meetings taking place on Sundays (and maybe on additional feast days). A 'church' is a place where such formal meetings take place, and Christians 'go to church'. The meetings themselves have been formal and structured, following a set liturgy from which there is little or no deviation. Some at least of those who attend these meetings do so precisely because they find the undeviating formula reassuring.

The theory was that that everyone in the local community should attend these meetings. In former years, most European societies had means of social control to encourage that in practice, though one wonders how effective they were. Certainly when an official church census was taken in England and Wales at the end of March 1851, Victorians were shocked to find that in many places less than half the population attended a place of worship on the Sunday concerned. Since then, the position has only become worse. Elsewhere in this book, we have given figures for church attendance which suggest that in north and west Europe often less than 10% of those who identify as Christians attend church. The figures are a little higher in southern countries like Spain and Italy, but just as low as in Orthodox Russia.

The evidence is that modern Europeans do not in general like formal church services. That is not surprising when the form is compared with, for example, television and radio programmes with their mixture of short and varied contributions—they give the appearance of being informal and spontaneous, even if they are carefully choreographed throughout by editors and producers who have the technology to whisper in the ear of the presenter who appears to be in charge. When much of the populace do attend a large gathering, it is a sporting event or a pop concert, both of which appeal to the participants' senses with a razzle-dazzle of different acts and activities (with sporting events more and more having to imitate pop-concerts). We should note, however, that the direction of travel of entertainment is that it takes place in the home via the internet.

We should honour these trends in our mission activities, and in shaping our church activities as well (while recognising that the latter are attracting a smaller and smaller segment of society). Informality is crucial in the structure of our activities as well as our dress. And the small group in the home (or on the internet) is informal and facilitates, even encourages, dialogue as the form of teaching. It also allows for eating together which, even more than in earlier decades, is the characteristic leisure activity of Europeans—that too is less formal in character than it used to be at least in upper-and middle-class settings. This should not trouble us as the church that emerges in the pages of the New Testament focussed on informal, almost impromptu, gatherings centred on food. If we are Christians who hold that there is something authorititative about the practice of the New Testament church, we should be capable of adapting our activities and methods to the needs of modern Europe (remembering always that what is appropriate in France or Sweden may not be so in Romania).

Music

It seems likely that popular music (differing in character according to place and time) has been an important feature in all human cultures. It is a field of activity in which what is judged to be of quality tends to be preserved as part of the corpus of quality or classical music, while the character of popular music is forgotten from generation to generation, at least until the nineteenth century. But popular music became of special significance in European culture in the twentieth century. It seems to be a Euro-American phenomenon, yet it has penetrated worldwide, in some societies as an alternative, underground activity which the young relish to the annoyance of (perhaps in order to annoy) older generations. We should not underestimate the significance of popular music (and related events like music festivals) pretty well for all generations and classes in Europe today. Among other things, popular music is an important purveyor of ideas and moral values, and of latter-day romanticism.

Very much because of the role of popular music in shaping morality and popular consciousness, evangelism would be wise to take cognizance of it, and ask how music can and should be used to communicate ideas and the gospel itself in different cultural settings across Europe. If we do not, we may be missing a way of communicating which is of real significance among present-day Europeans. As a result, our evangelism may be stunted.

Social media

Another challenge in gospel communication may be electronic communication and in particular social media. There is no doubt that in the past thirty years, they have emerged as a new facet of communication and influence which we shall neglect in evangelism at our peril. An obvious consideration is that many young people, perhaps throughout Europe, only receive information and communicate electronically: it is their tool of choice for education, for informing themselves, for entertaining themselves, and for communicating with others. If we want to communicate with young people (which of us would not wish to?), we have to learn how to use electronic means to best effect. We also need to recruit young people to do it, and to allow them the freedom to do it.

Having reflected on these important issues, in the next chapter we want to drill down a little further by reminding ourselves of the different kinds of people who live in today's Europe (as described in chapter 1). We will briefly think about some of the intellectual challenges that may hold them back from faith and explore some of the answers we can give.

Chapter 7

Getting a hearing for the gospel

I suspect all of us have taken part in conversations where we were speaking to someone and getting the feeling they were not understanding us. Whether it was a glazed look in their eyes or a question they asked, we realised we weren't getting through. Evangelism can be a bit like that. We can be sharing the gospel, but the person we are talking to has not comprehended what we are saying. For this reason, our presentation of the gospel has to be nuanced so as to speak in a way that the person can genuinely understand.

When it comes to evangelism in Europe, this is absolutely the case. We stated in chapter 1 that Europe is not a monolith, but rather a patchwork of different worldviews, all of which were embedded over a long period of history. This is partly a question of knowing and understanding the history and culture of the *particular* country in which we are evangelising. But also, to be effective in evangelism, we need to reflect again on the *different kinds* of people who live in Europe, irrespective of national boundaries, and ask, how are we to communicate to them? To give a simple illustration, it is unnecessary to try to convince a European Muslim that God exists—it is a question of diplomatically introducing him or her to attributes of God that are revealed in Scripture. But a secularist atheist would need to be convinced of the existence of God. Before we do so, I will give the same warning that I did at the end of chapter 1. People are often complex individuals from complex backgrounds. The general differences identified in chapter 1 are real, and many people will not fit neatly into just one category. So, while we may major on one particular area of discussion in evangelism, we will have to use a wider array of discussion points to communicate fully with the person.

We begin by thinking about religious Europeans and how we might begin to influence them with the gospel. This group includes Roman Catholics, Lutherans, Orthodox, Reformed, Anglicans, and some liberalised Protestants. Although these churches are generally in decline in Europe, they still have a significant presence and influence on general thought, public life and commentary. A challenge that we face as we try to share the gospel with them is that of nominalism. Many people who say they are, for example, Catholic or Orthodox, might not attend church with any kind of regularity and are at best apathetic. They may only have a superficial understanding of their church's teaching, and their thought may owe more to that of society around them. However, if they have been baptised as infants and consider themselves to be a 'good person', they will probably feel that that is enough and that they are Christian, whatever that word actually means to them. Others, of course, are much more committed to their faith and willing to debate with anyone who would try to evangelise them. In either case, we need to be clear about what we communicate to them.

Responding to religious Europeans

The first thing we need to do is to be careful about our attitude. Criticising or ridiculing another person's belief system is neither gracious nor effective. We should, of course, seek to dismantle false beliefs, but this should be done graciously and we should rely on the Holy Spirit to convict through the Word of God. We need to learn the skill of sharing biblical truth without their switching off.

Secondly, focus on the centrality of Scripture. Most Catholic, Orthodox, and Reformed Christians believe the Bible to be of special significance in spiritual terms, so we have a basis for discussion. We will also have to confront the issue of religious 'tradition' at some point and the only authority we can have to do that is Scripture.

Thirdly, we need to stick to the Bible's salvation storyline and keep the main thing the main thing. We must not be diverted into side arguments or fine points of doctrine. What is relevant is that all have sinned, even religious people, and the only hope of salvation is faith in the finished work of Christ (as the Eucharist which they usually value so clearly demonstrates).

I am not suggesting that this is a simple thing to do. Years ago on a GLO team in Italy, I had a conversation with a Catholic gentleman. He was polite and sincere, but when I had shared the gospel with him using Scripture, he replied by saying that his priest, who to him represented the church, thought differently and therefore I must be wrong. This was frustrating, but we must stick to Scripture and pray that the Holy Spirit will break through such barriers.

Similarities and differences

Engaging with religious Europeans brings its own challenges. To begin with, as many Catholics and Orthodox believers see themselves as Christians, they may question why we seem to be assuming that they are not Christians and wish to convert them. On one mission in Malta, I was invited by a Roman Catholic Charismatic group to join them for an open-air worship service. Their music was familiar and their liturgy certainly exalted Christ. While leading a mission team in Hungary, I was also invited by the minister of a liberal Reformed church to work with his church in reaching the local town. These situations arose because of my attempts to get alongside Roman Catholics and liberal Protestants so that I could witness to them. It was clear I had a choice to make and the stakes were high because there was the potential for offence. No doubt, some of these people had a genuine relationship with Christ; others however were just religious. Situations like these are not easy and there is no perfect way of dealing with them.

That said, we need to keep two things in balance. First, we need to ensure that we do nothing that detracts from our presentation of the gospel. Secondly, we need to remember that Jesus mixed freely with people and spent time with them. He both accepted the invitation from Simon the Pharisee and ate with the tax collectors and sinners; he worshipped in the Temple; he recognised the faith of the Gentile centurion; and he spoke to the Samaritan woman at the well—in all cases without himself sinning. This kind of incarnated ministry should be our model and will require a commitment to get alongside people where they are and make the Christian faith real to them.

If we can keep this balance and use every opportunity to communicate the gospel clearly, we can speak effectively into the lives of even the most religious

Europeans. Of course, in all this we are dependent on the work of the Holy Spirit to convict people of sin and their need of a Saviour.

Thinking about Enlightenment Europeans

Although Christianity (in its broadest sense) remains influential in Europe and finds expression through institutions like the Roman Catholic and Orthodox Churches, it is nevertheless on the decline. Since the Enlightenment, religious Europeans have come to be rivalled by their secular and non-religious counterparts, that is, Europeans who put their faith in human reason, not God's revelation.

This group is not a monolith: those within it come in many different shades. They include committed atheists and agnostics, as well as the many Europeans who may even label themselves as 'Christian', but never attend church or harbour any religious beliefs, or who have simply adopted a secularist way of thinking. The latter may not argue against the existence of God, but they have no conviction that God must exist and don't think that religion has anything to offer. They may appreciate the beauty of Christian art and music but, for them, the church is just some sort of museum or a social club for those who wish to indulge.

Why do people question?

Many Enlightenment Europeans have questions about religious claims and there are often reasons for this. First, they think that science has provided explanations for the universe and for life, and consequently think that a creator God is unnecessary. Secondly, there is a common belief that science and faith are inevitably in conflict. This is of course untrue, but widely believed none the less.

What is more, the Judaeo-Christian worldview in general, and confidence in Scripture in particular, has diminished and even broken down in broader culture over the past couple of centuries. As a result, the importance and accuracy of the Bible has been challenged.

An even bigger issue is the problem of suffering which has been a thorny issue for humankind since The Fall. The existence of suffering, which we see daily on our TV screens, has caused many Europeans to question whether there is a God and, if there is one, why does he not put an end to it all?

Learning to witness

How do we begin witnessing to those who claim to be atheists and believe the Bible is just a book of superstitious myths, or is simply false? We can often begin by exposing the weakness of their philosophy. This may involve raising serious questions about the origin of the universe and of life, neither of which can be adequately explained by an atheistic worldview. Atheists often accuse Christians of being anti-scientific, but this is false. The truth is that many of the founding fathers of science such as Leonardo Da Vinci, Blaise Pascal, Sir Isaac Newton, Michael Faraday and William Thompson were Christians. Moreover, their study of science enhanced their faith because they expected to observe order in God's creation.

The religion of evolution

Some atheists appeal to evolution as if it were a silver bullet that slays religion. But the theory of evolution, as often presented in this argument, begs as many questions as it claims to provide answers for. It is ill-equipped to explain why the DNA found in every human cell is so information rich. Equally, it cannot explain the existence of matter, the fine tuning of the universe, or the human capacity to appreciate beauty or morality. The truth is that evolution is as much a belief system as Christianity. There is also a growing amount of research that undermines the credibility of evolutionary theory, as well as a growing number of scientists who simply do not accept evolution as a given.[1]

However, this is only half the battle. We should also give positive reasons for believing in the existence of God, as well as demonstrating that belief in God is actually a very attractive thing. After all, we live in a society where loneliness, hopelessness, despair and even suicide are commonplace. This is not because we are poor or lack education, but because many feel life is simply not worth living. It is here that the Christian message can have a real impact. It is good news for those who feel oppressed, as Jesus offers relief from guilt,

---

1. For further reading on all the arguments discussed in this chapter, see Appendix D below (pp. 163–4).

a purpose in life, as well as meaning, significance and hope. This point must be enthusiastically emphasized, so that the atheist can see that Christianity is not just credible, but also desirable.

Dealing with agnostics

Not all Enlightenment Europeans are atheists; some just have serious questions about faith. Some are questions about the reliability of the Bible which was written a very long time ago by people with whom we have no direct link. Moreover, the original documents have long since been destroyed, and so all we have now is copies of copies, which raises questions about whether the text can be trusted? Others have questions about the content of the Bible, for example, the miracles of Jesus, including the Resurrection; or the moral credentials of the way in which God is often depicted as acting in the Old Testament. Many more will question whether belief in God is consistent with the suffering in the world.

The truth is that the list of questions and doubts which people have is almost endless, though only some of them are real obstacles to believing. So how do we tackle them and share the gospel effectively?

First, we must take people's doubts seriously. Some Christians mistakenly think that when non-Christians raise intellectual questions, it is simply because they want to avoid accepting their sin and their spiritual status before God. This is not my experience. On the contrary, many people have doubts about Christianity and, when they voice them, it is often because they are honest people who want to find the answer.

That people have doubts should not surprise us, given that we believe in a God whom we cannot see, touch, smell or hear. We believe that salvation comes as a result of something that happened 2,000 years ago. Moreover, we share the message with people who are spiritually blind and have grown up in a secular culture that denies the spiritual; and they have gone through an education system that prizes rationality and empirical science. All of this gives good reason for thinking people to ask searching questions. If we really love people, we should be willing to take their questions seriously and help them find answers.

Secondly, we need to encourage sceptics to search the Bible honestly and sincerely, to discover truth. If someone is genuinely seeking, the Bible can speak to them and they can find the truth, even if they have significant intellectual questions that need to be answered along the way.

Thinking about Emergent Europeans

We now think of Europeans who have been shaped by postmodernism and have lost confidence in the objectivity of truth and ethics. These are 'Emergent Europeans'.[2] Previous generations of Europeans believed that truth was the same truth for everyone, and may also have believed that God was the guarantor of truth. For Emergent Europeans, truth is personal and subjective: it is truth for you and may differ from what is truth for others. Many also have a tendency to see Christian belief as somewhat dogmatic and intolerant, especially with respect to topics that they care about like sexual ethics and gender. And they can be as concerned about the flaws of science (such as industrial pollution and nuclear weaponry) as they are aware of its benefits.

This questioning of truth has been supercharged by the advent of the global village and mass media. People are bombarded with cultures, ideas and value systems of peoples from all over the world, and, when they are compared to Western culture and values, the West is often found wanting. Increasingly, we are developing an eclectic culture into which any value or idea can easily be assimilated. Truth is merely a matter of opinion, not an expression of what is real and actual.

Downgrading of deity

Another feature of Emergents is that God is not central to anything or even worth arguing about. If someone chooses to believe in God, that is up to them, but this cannot be a universal reality. God is not the transcendent Lord of the universe: he is more of a hobby if you are into that kind of thing, rather like football or music, and no one should expect everyone to believe in their particular god.

Of course, spirituality itself is not rejected; indeed, tarot cards, crystals and reading star signs are as popular as ever. People are also drawn to the kind of

---

2. See page 16 above.

mass spirituality which happens at events such as music festivals, celebrity funerals, and pagan rituals. The difference is that these forms of spirituality are not sustained by any concept of objective truth. Indeed, it does not really matter to participants whether what they are doing is even logical. That it is experience-orientated and enjoyable by them is enough!

Relativized morality

The questioning of absolutes has reduced all behaviours to the level of a lifestyle choice. If someone chooses to have a relationship with someone of their own sex, to use recreational drugs or foul language, to transition into their chosen gender or no gender at all, to terminate their unborn child, or to live in an open marriage, we cannot and should not condemn them because there is no objective moral yardstick to judge their actions. Anyone who dares to condemn is dismissed as an intolerant bigot.

The media tend to support this new moral freedom. Talk show hosts, comedians, actors and pop stars, and indeed any celebrities, are the new arbiters of morality. If Gary Lineker, Taylor Swift or James Corden declares something to be morally right, it must be! In practice, this means that morality is reduced to its lowest common denominator. As long as no one is hurt and Mother Nature is undamaged, anything goes!

Pluralism

What is true for morals is also true of religion. No one faith can claim to be true in an absolute sense, only true for the individual. Though Europe is considered nominally Christian, in reality Christianity occupies the same space on the shelves of the spiritual supermarket as any other religion. All religions are considered equal, and equally true—except that it seems that Christianity is reserved for special condemnation.

The net result of this is that, in much of European society, the Bible carries no real authority. While religious Europeans may claim that the Bible is 'the Word of God', most Emergent Europeans are at least slightly sceptical of it and, when pushed, would not be able to say whether or not they see the Bible as being essentially different from the Koran or the Bhagavad Gita or any other human publication.

Experience

A further trait is their orientation towards feeling and experience. Facts have been replaced by feelings and truth by experience. Just as Nietzsche believed that an idea did not need to be true as long as it is 'life-affirming', so contemporary Europeans believe that 'If it feels good, do it!' Life is built not on objective truths, but on experiences. Actions are judged not on objective morality, but on whether we enjoy the experience of living.

This desire for experience can be seen in 'retail therapy', and a culture in which buying things for their usefulness is less important than the brand image. It can be seen in the vast diversity of music and media, as well as in politics where image and sound-bite are more potent vote-winners than are substance and policy.[3]

Among these Europeans, God is largely irrelevant, Scripture carries no weight, people are confused by many religious options, and believe that there is no sin, except that of believing something to be absolutely true.

Witnessing to Emergent Europeans

How do we even begin to reach Emergent Europeans? In my experience, they are the hardest group of people to reach because a great deal of work has to be done before we can get down to discussing the truthfulness and coherence of the Christian worldview. This is because for Emergent Europeans, the starting point is the question of truth itself.

The truth sets you free

Truth is vital in evangelism, because the gospel is not just good news: it is actually true! For many Emergents, truth is a difficult notion to grasp.[4] Given this, perhaps we can come up with a simple (maybe simplistic) definition of truth. Truth could be described as a belief which can be tested.[5] When this is

---

3. It goes without saying that all of these traits, as well as the four categories of people outlined, can equally be seen in other parts of the world, not least in North America and Australasia. However, the focus of this book is on Europe and the description given fits Europe at least as well as, if not better than, it does anywhere else in the West

4. Peter Hicks, *Truth: Could it be True?* (Solway, 1996), p. 211.

5. It must be noted that this is also a limited definition because the word 'tested' is open to ambiguities; however it does function as a useful starting definition for the purposes of evangelism.

applied to Christianity, we are able to demonstrate, not only that truth exists, but Christianity can be demonstrated to be the truth.

Of course, just because someone claims not to believe in truth, it does not follow that this is actually the case. Sometimes in conversation it can be useful to ask what issues they are passionate about and what issues they think other people should be passionate about. It can very quickly dawn on them that there are indeed things which they believe really are true.

Critiquing pluralism

Once truth is demonstrated to exist, we need to deal with philosophical barriers that might prevent emergent thinkers from believing in Christ. However, removing these barriers is only the beginning, because many people come to believe in the essential truthfulness of the Christian gospel, yet do not go on to trust Christ. What is needed is the conviction of sin which the Holy Spirit alone can bring. However, the removal of these barriers is an essential starting point, because a person will not become a Christian if he or she believes that there are genuine reasons for not accepting Christ.

This brings us to pluralism—the belief that all religions lead to God and are of equal truthfulness and value. This is a significant issue with Emergent Europeans and they will often argue that religious beliefs are culturally conditioned. In other words, a Pakistani Muslim believes what he does because he comes from Pakistan, and an American Christian believes what she does because she comes from the USA. Their beliefs are due solely to their background, not a conscious choice based on truth.

This argument does not actually work because something is not necessarily true just because some people may practise it as part of their culture. For example, witchcraft, child sacrifice and cannibalism should not be accepted as true and acceptable simply because they are practised in some cultures. Truth needs to have a better foundation.

We need to point out that religious pluralism is inherently unworkable, because the religious pluralist cannot have his cake and eat it. By stating that there is no absolute truth, the pluralist is actually making a statement which is, by implication, an absolute truth, thus refuting the proposition that there is no absolute truth.[6]

Deductive logic

Suppose I were teaching an art class on the use of colour. I show the class two large pieces of card, one red, the other blue. As I deliver the lecture, I claim that the two pieces of card are actually the same colour. The class is surprised because they know what red and blue are and that they are different. However, I persist and try to convince them that it would be 'politically correct' and 'tolerant' to claim that the two cards are the same colour and, as the emergent generation do not believe in absolutes, I insist my statements can be true. Despite my insistence, the class cannot accept that two colours that are clearly different can actually be the same colour, because it is simply illogical!

The same logic can be applied to how we view different religions. It is absurd to claim that they are all basically the same, however attractive such a position appears to be. The reality is that every religion claims that it is true. Moreover, religions differ radically from each other, and any similarities are small and relatively insignificant. We see this when comparing Christianity, Hinduism, Buddhism, Shintoism and Islam.

These faiths account for more than half of the world's population and, when viewed carefully, their differences are so great that they cannot find common ground, even in their definition of who God is. Muslims are monotheists, people who see God as a single entity. Christians, on the other hand, while believing God is one, see him in the three persons of Father, Son and Holy Spirit. Hindus cannot agree among themselves as to what they believe about God. Some believe in one god, others in millions of gods, while others are pantheistic. Buddhism, on the other hand, is a non-theistic, if not atheistic, religion.

The same is true when it comes to the person of Jesus Christ. Muslims and Christians have a belief system that includes Jesus, but Christians claim he is the incarnate Son of God, while Muslims claim that this is blasphemous

---

6. A useful exposition can be found in Norman Geisler, *Baker Encyclopedia of Christian Apologetics* (Ada MI: Baker, 1998), p. 745.

and that he is no more than a great prophet.[7] Christians also believe in the resurrection of Jesus, while Muslims deny that Jesus even died.

Jesus claimed to be the author of life and the only way to the Father. Jesus also claimed to be the one who gives resurrection and eternal life, a concept very different from the Hindu idea of reincarnation. In all these ways, these religions sharply differ, so we do not have the luxury of saying that all religions are basically the same. In the light of these fundamental diferences, it is also strange to claim that all religions are of equal value as ways to God.

Sincerity does not make something true

When faced with this reality, many Emergent Europeans will bring up the issue of the sincerity of people of other faiths and insist that God would not condemn such a sincere person. At this point, the issue can become quite emotive as the assertion needs to be challenged.

One way of doing so is to point out that, centuries ago, the Flat Earth Society came into being, claiming the earth to be flat. Subsequently, scientific observation had demonstrated this to be false; yet the society still exists and insists the earth is flat. The fact is they are wrong and that that does not change simply because they are sincere. By the same token, religious sincerity does not make a belief true.

Having demonstrated that pluralism is intellectually bankrupt, we are now in a position to present the truthfulness of Christianity. This can be done in at least two ways: first, presenting the Bible as the revelation of God's truth; and secondly, by focussing our hearer's attention on the person of Jesus Christ.

An inspired book

The reason we might begin with a defence of the Bible is that what we believe about Jesus is found there and, if the Bible can be demonstrated to be true, we will have a platform from which to declare the uniqueness of Christ. We need to emphasize that the Bible is inspired (2 Tim. 3: 16: 'All Scripture is inspired'[8]), which means that what we have on the page are not just the

---

7. Harold Netland, *Encountering Religious Pluralism: The Challenge to Christian Faith & Mission* (Downers Grove IL: InterVarsity, 2001), p. 182.

8. Some translations use the words 'God breathed'; see also 2 Peter 1: 21.

thoughts of some human author, but of God himself. Jesus ascribed authority to the Bible and demanded that we take it seriously.

One of the evidences of the authority of Scripture is the fulfilment of biblical prophecy. For example, there were prophecies made in the Old Testament about the coming of the Messiah that Jesus fulfilled.[9] They make a compelling case for seeing the Bible as the unique Word of God.

Reliability of the text

Even given this evidence, some might still have doubts about the reliability of the Bible. This is the moment to point out that the Bible is not just a religious text that seeks to explain something about God, but it is also a book that is grounded in history and in real events. The book of Exodus, for example, records actual events and the author, Moses, was a participant in some of those events and therefore a good eyewitness. Likewise in the New Testament, writers such as Luke remind us that the material that we read is real evidence that has been carefully compiled from testimony of eyewitnesses. (Lk. 1: 1–4).

Added to this is corroborating evidence deduced from the context of the biblical record. Christianity emerged in Jerusalem shortly after the death and resurrection of Jesus Christ. Acts 2 states that Christians openly proclaimed in the public arena their beliefs about controversial doctrines such as the resurrection in the presence of both friendly and hostile witnesses. The Gospels were also circulated in the context of hostile witnesses, many of whom would have been around when the events recorded in them took place. Despite all of this, we find no contemporary refuting any of the claims in the Gospels or Acts, which strongly suggests the reliability of these accounts.

Not only can we be confident that the claims made in the Bible are credible and true, but also that the copies we have of the Bible books are a faithful reproduction of the original text. When it comes to the Old Testament, we can have this confidence because we know a great deal about the copying techniques and know that they were reliable enough to give us a faithful text. But more than that, we have alternative texts that we can use as a comparison. The standard text used to translate the Old Testament is the Masoretic Text which

---

9. And the total number of biblical prophecies runs into hundreds.

was produced by the Masoretes, one of the copying communities. But we also have the Dead Sea Scrolls which are 1,000 years older than the Masoretic Texts and, when the two texts are examined together, we can demonstrate that the copying techniques proved reliable over that 1,000-year period. This is not surprising, as the copiers revered the text and knew the importance of what they were doing.

When it comes to the New Testament, we can have equal confidence. This is, first, because we have more ancient texts in existence (25,000) than for any other document of the ancient world.[10] However, numbers alone do not tell the full story. Scholars are able to scrutinise these documents using sophisticated tests and demonstrate the accuracy and faithfulness of the transmission with a high degree of accuracy. This shows that, not only is the Bible grounded in real history, but the copying processes were robust: we can be certain that we have what was written.

DOCUMENT	NO. OF COPIES	EARLIEST COPIES	TIME SPAN
New Testament	25,000	200 AD 114 AD (fragment)	100 YEARS
Caesar	10	900 AD	1,000 YEARS
Plato	7	900 AD	1,300 YEARS
Homer	643	400 BC	400 YEARS

The credibility of the Bible can further be validated by archaeology and other ancient works. Archaeology provides hard evidence that claims made in the Bible are consistent with what we know about the ancient world. Donald Wiseman, a former departmental head at the British Museum, stated that, at the time that he wrote, some 25,000 archaeological sites relating to biblical

---

10. This includes over 5,000 Greek manuscripts, 10,000 Latin Vulgate manuscripts, and more than 9,000 other early versions (Josh McDowell, *The New Evidence that Demands a Verdict* (Thomas Nelson Publishers, 1999), p. 34. Note also Bruce Metzger, *The Text of the New Testament,* Chapter 2, 'Important Witnesses to the Text of the New Testament' (Oxford: Clarendon Press, 1985), pp. 36–92.

times had been uncovered.[11] None of these had brought into question the events, places or people mentioned in the Bible.

Other ancient writings provide corroborative evidence of the claims of Scripture. Writings like the works of Josephus, or the Jewish Tanna'im (repeaters of tradition) which date from AD70 and AD200 respectively, or the Baritha, confirm many New Testament claims. For example, in them we read about Jesus and the controversy which he caused within the Jewish establishment. It even tells us that Jesus was crucified on the eve of the Passover, which is exactly what John's Gospel tells us.[12] We have compelling reason to hold that the Bible is credible. Sir Fredrick Kenyon, a renowned expert on ancient texts, spent a lifetime studying the Bible and concluded, 'The Christian can take the whole Bible in his hand and say without fear or hesitation that he holds in it the true Word of God, handed down without essential loss from generation to generation throughout the centuries'.[13]

The Bible is not only a life-changing book; it is also one that can be historically validated and accepted as reliable. Given the solid track-record that the Bible presents, even the most doubting sceptic can be presented with compelling evidence for believing in it. Moreover, while other religious texts do exist, they simply cannot be validated in the same robust way.

The transcendent Christ

Having defended the Bible with our emergent friends, we can also argue for the credibility of Christ. This is important in a pluralist culture, because it is the uniqueness of Christ that makes Christianity unique. The word unique is overused but, when used of Jesus, it absolutely fits. For a start, virgin birth is not a claim made of the founders of other world religions. Then there is his moral purity which his adversaries could not deny. The same could not be said of Mohammed, Buddha or even Krishna.[14] Indeed, their own scriptures admit

11. Donald Wiseman, cited in Steve Kumar, *Christianity for Sceptics: An Understandable Examination of Christian Belief* (Grand Rapids MI: Hendricksen, 2000), p. 111.

12. F. F. Bruce, *Jesus and Christian Origins Outside the New Testament* (London: Hodder & Stoughton, 1974), pp. 55–6.

13. Frederic G. Kenyon, *Our Bible and the Ancient Manuscripts* (London 1895—available in facsimile reprint from Wipf & Stock, Eugene OR), p. 23.

14. *Jesus among other Gods*, p. 40.

to this. The Koran informs us that Mohammed had to ask for forgiveness for his sin or face death. The Bhagavad Gita describes the immoral life of Krishna, while the many reincarnations of the Buddha presuppose his sinfulness. Then we have the miracles of Jesus which can be historically attested, as they were done in a public setting in the presence of hostile witnesses.[15] No other founder of a religion can make this claim.[16]

We also note that Jesus actually claimed to be God (Jn. 10: 30), claimed to forgive sin (Mt. 9: 1–8), judge the world (Jn. 5: 27, 30), and give eternal life (Jn. 3: 16). This means that we must either dismiss him as delusional, or take his claims seriously. In the words of C. S. Lewis, Jesus was either, 'a megalomaniac compared with whom Hitler was the most sane and humble of men' or 'a complete lunatic suffering from that form of delusion which undermines the whole mind of man, or he was indeed God'.[17]

Most important of all, he rose from the dead. This truth is made all the more remarkable because Jesus predicted it (Mt. 16: 21). The claim of the resurrection is not merely a Christian belief, but one which can be demonstrated to be true by articulating four independently verifiable facts.

First, that Jesus died at the hands of professional executioners and that the historical description of his death gives evidence for its reality.[18] Secondly, he was buried in the tomb of a high-profile individual by the name of Joseph of Arimathea. Thirdly, the tomb was found to be empty with no credible explanation other than a resurrection.[19] And fourthly, following the resurrection, Jesus repeatedly appeared to a wide variety of people and then these sightings stopped abruptly.[20]

---

15. These are taken from a longer list of reasons found in Bernard Ramm, *Protestant Christian Evidences* (Chicago IL: Moody Press. 1953), pp. 140–143.

16. Some might dispute this claim, insisting that other founders like Mohammed performed miracles. However, the alleged miracles of Mohammed are neither of the calibre of Jesus' miracles, nor can they be tested. As William Craig points out, they were not claimed by either Mohammed or the Koran; rather they are a later and unverifiable tradition (Lee Strobel, *The Case for Faith: A Journalist Investigates the Toughest Questions* (London: Harper Collins, 2000), pp. 70, 71.

17. C. S. Lewis, *God in the Dock: Essays on Theology and Ethics* (London: Font, 1983), p. 88.

18. Josh McDowell, *The New Evidence that Demands a Verdict*, p. 224.

19. William Lane Craig provides a compelling defence of the resurrection, citing both the historical reliability of the texts and the individual components of the case: *Apologetics: An Introduction* (Chicago IL: Moody Press, 1984), pp. 167–206.

20. Paul E. Little, *Know Why you Believe* (Downers Grove IL: IVP, 4th ed., 2000), p. 54.

The sheer physicality of these appearances (Jn. 20: 26–31; 21: 1–23) also ground them in reality. This too makes him unique, because the other founders of world religions are dead. His uniqueness forces us to give credence to his statement that he is the 'way and the truth and the life' and 'No-one comes to the Father except through me' (Jn. 14: 6).

Thinking about the New Europeans

The final group are the New Europeans, people from all ethnic backgrounds and faiths who are now part of European society. This group will continue to grow, not least because Europe's ageing population necessitates ongoing immigration.[21] While many of the New Europeans are Christian, many are also Muslim. Under different scenarios for migration of Muslims to Europe, the population of Muslims in Europe could rise from 26m in 2016 to 36m (with zero Muslim migration) to 58m with medium migration, and 76m with high migration. Under the medium migration scenarios between a sixth and a fifth of the populations of the UK, France and Sweden could be Muslim. (The likely growth in the number of immigrants is part of the background to the swing in policy across Europe to restricting migration.)[22]

How do we reach Muslims or other religious groups for Christ? One of the problems that we face is that some of these 'ethnic' communities are not well integrated into mainstream European life and are often 'ghettoised'. We therefore need to befriend them in order to earn the right to speak. Some Christians feel threatened by people from other faiths, and especially by Muslims. In part, this is fear of the unknown, but it is also fear generated by the negative images that many people have of Muslims. The reality is that, although there are radicalised elements in Islam as well as in all world religions, the majority of the world's religious people are ordinary humans who are struggling to find their way in life. If we approach them humbly and with love

---

21. It is interesting that *Time Magazine* reported that Western governments have tried to combat the crisis with pension and labour reform, but have shied away from urging people to have more babies (November 2004, p. 44).

22. 'Europe's Growing Muslim Population', Report by the Pew Research Group, November 2017 (https://www.pewresearch.org/religion/2017/11/29/europes-growing-muslim-population/, accessed on 3.2.24). According to, mainly, Pew Research Centre figures, there were in around 2016 about 4.5 million Muslims in Germany, 5.7 million in France, 2.1 million in the UK, and 3 million in Italy.

and friendship, they are more likely to respond positively. A Christian who is kind, practical and neighbourly will ultimately earn the trust of his Muslim or Hindu neighbour.

We also need to live a godly life in front of them. Whenever we tell someone that we are Christians, they begin to scrutinise us, to see if what we claim to believe makes a difference to how we live. Many Muslim and Hindu immigrants are appalled by the immorality that they see in Europe and, given that they think of Europe as a Christian continent, this colours their view of Christianity. If they can see how Christianity is really lived out, they will be more willing to listen.

From a practical point of view, we should also remember the power of community and the peer pressure that people of other faiths face. We need to patiently help them to take small steps towards believing in Christ. This is further complicated by the fact that most religions do not simply embody a set of doctrines, but an entire culture and way of life as well. The process of sharing the gospel cannot be rushed.

What do I say?

Having thought about our approach, what should we actually say? It is difficult to be specific here, because every religion is unique, as is every individual worshipper; so there is no standard approach that works.[23] What we can do, however, is reflect on some of the key points to be taken into account if our evangelism is to be successful.

First, it can be helpful to state that Christianity is not a Western religion, because, in the minds of our listeners, there is often a connection between a geographical region, or a political standpoint, and faith. We need to emphasize that Christianity did not originate in the West, and that it is growing most quickly in the non-Western world.

Secondly, we need to stress that God can be personally known. This is a difficult point to establish, or to be accepted, especially when dealing with a religion that is as confused about God as Hinduism, or one in which God is

---

23. The practicalities of evangelism in the developed world are dealt with extensively in Martin Erwin & Stephen McQuoid (ed's), *Making Jesus Known Today and Tomorrow: Spreading the Gospel in Twenty-First Century Britain* (Westbury, Wilts: Counties, 2023).

distant as in Islam. Nevertheless, the knowability of God is a vital component in our presentation, because we all have an innate spirituality, or a God-shaped void. If a religious person calls out sincerely to God, they will find he is not distant, but personal, and a loving father.

Thirdly, we need to stress the sinfulness of humanity. Most people, when pressed, will admit that their lives are not as they should be, and we should also pray that the Holy Spirit will prick their consciences, so as to make them instinctively aware of their own fallenness.

Fourthly, we should always be prepared and willing to ask questions. It shows a desire to understand the person and it helps them to think about their own faith. However, we should put questions in a gentle and gracious manner, rather than the aggressive way that it is all too easy to adopt in discussion.

Finally, we need to raise the matters of forgiveness and eternal life through Jesus. This is the heart of the Christian message, and we need to ensure that it is these, and not side issues, that dominate our evangelistic conversations.

Of course, none of these guarantee a response from any sort of European. Evangelism is never easy, and we need the power of the Holy Spirit, working through us and convicting our listeners of their sin and the truth of the gospel. But, through prayer and gracious interaction, even the hardest people can be won for Jesus Christ.

In the next chapter we will start to think about some of the practical questions that we need to addresss as we commit ourselves to reaching Europe for Christ.

Chapter 8

Preparing for the task

You may remember the first time that you were behind the wheel of a car, to start to learn to drive. It is an exciting but daunting prospect, and any new driver quickly realises that there is a lot to learn. It is also necessary to keep your nerve, because learning to drive a car is a genuine challenge.

We have been thinking about the great diversity of Europe as a mission field and also about some of the challenges if we want to reach these many countries for Christ. We now need to ask the question, how will the job be done? The answer necessarily falls into several parts. The first is, what kind of people will be effective in reaching Europeans for Christ?

What kind of people?

Mission is challenging wherever it is, but nowhere more so than in Europe today. While God can use anyone who is willing, there are certainly character strengths that will be very useful.

The first is **tenacity**. This will be needed because the reality is that the vast bulk of Europeans are not particularly interested in the gospel or indeed in any faith. Secularism is so pronounced across much of Europe that, even when you come across people who are friendly and happy to talk, most of them will be reticent to talk about their spiritual lives because that is a private space that they are accustomed to think should not be invaded. I remember having a conversation with a friend who had, as a missionary to an Islamic majority country in the 10/40 window, planted a church over a period of 20 years. On his return to the UK, his home church asked him to take charge of the evangelism programme as he was clearly so experienced. It was some months later that we had our conversation, and he was clearly agitated. He told me that, in the country where he served as a missionary, it was very easy to begin a gospel conversation because, even though the locals argued and debated with him, they wanted to discuss God and thought that personal belief was important. However, he found people in the UK unresponsive and getting gospel conversations going was so difficult that he was beginning to lose confidence in his ability as an evangelist.

This experience could be found all over Europe. It is a tough mission field and therefore one that requires tenacity to keep going in sharing the gospel openly, as so many people do not want to know.

Linked with this, it is important that people working in Europe are **relational**. Most of the evangelism will need to be informal and through friendship, especially at the early stages. Europe is not the sort of place where, if you advertise an evangelistic event, people will just turn up. It is more a place where spiritual conversations happen in the context of a trusting relationship. Willingness to get to know people, to be friendly and relational, and to have an open home, are of great benefit. Christians wanting to make an impact will need to be willing to give time to relationship-building, to be with people and love them without being judgmental. In most European countries, including the United Kingdom, there is such a huge gap between church culture and the average man or woman in the street that effective evangelism will necessitate crossing that divide, so that people can see that Christians are normal people who are just like them.

It is also important to **know what you are talking about**. This may be an obvious point, but many Europeans have been blessed with a good level of education and some European cultures prize it, love their history, and are philosophically astute. When serious spiritual conversations occur, many people are questioning and there is often a profound scepticism about Christian claims. I mentioned in chapter 1 that there are also many Europeans who come from other religious positions. It is therefore important to have some kind of grasp of other religious belief systems, especially Islam. It is not that every European whom you might meet is an intellectual, though some are. However, an important part of our task is to show that the gospel is credible and to provide satisfying reasons for belief; European listeners are often a hard group to convince. If we are ignorant about the world around us and especially about the claims of Christian theology, we will not be convincing. We need to be able to give reasonable answers to genuine questions, and to defend the plausibility of the Christian faith. Getting to a place where we can do this requires hard work and discipline.[1]

What kind of missionary?

The second part of our answer involves asking how we will find the army of people needed to reach Europe for Christ. This is a huge issue and again one that has a variety of different angles. We first need to consider the strategic difference between using long-term and short-term missionaries.

Short-term mission

In the second half of the twentieth century, short-term mission was born and came into its own. Mass transport became both plentiful and cheap, and then Europe opened up with the fall of the Iron Curtain in 1990. Organisations like OM and YWAM took full advantage of this, as did GLO. One of the earliest short-term mission teams that GLO organised left in 1975 when around 50 young people, mostly from Scotland, travelled to Rome for two weeks' evangelism, as part of the Catholic Church's Jubilee Year, and distributed a million leaflets in five different languages. Since those early days, GLO Europe has mobilised and sent out over 15,000 people on short-term mission teams. These have primarily been younger people, but the age spectrum has been very broad and has included many retired people. Teams have lasted anything from a couple of days to a couple of weeks and occasionally longer.

The range of work done by these teams has been very extensive. Over the years, literally millions of pieces of literature have been distributed. Teams have sold Bibles and correspondence courses, have done door-to-door work, and conducted open-air meetings. They have organised a range of community activities, have run English classes, children's meetings, youth clubs and sports activities. All these things have been designed to get the gospel across to as many people as possible. These teams have made a huge impact and many

---

1. Tilsley College has been preparing people for mission for nearly 50 years and if you have an interest in being trained for service please enquire: https://glo-europe.org/tilsleycollege/

people across Europe have become Christians as a result. Is this, then, how we reach Europe for Christ?

The answer is both yes and no. Yes, because short-term mission has a vital role to play in the evangelisation of Europe. It has been effective in the past and will continue to be in the future. It has also proved to be a pipeline leading people into long-term mission. However, there is more to it than this. Short-term mission takes us only so far, but it is limited and therefore only part of the answer.

Long-term mission

This brings us to long-term mission commitment. If Europe is to be reached, there is a great need for people to give their lives to the task and that involves being committed to mission in the long-term.

There are several reasons for this. First, being effective in mission means understanding the language and especially the culture of the host country. Simply attending a language school or having some school or university qualifications in that language is not enough. A missionary becomes fluent in a language by living with the people in their host country and speaking the language daily. Many missionaries have testified that they were in their host country for several years before they were really comfortable using the language. This obviously requires doing more than a few short-term teams or even an extended internship of a year or two. It takes a long-term commitment.

Abiding relationships, which are at the heart of a missionary's life, also require time. When I reflect on the relationships that I have with my own neighbours, they have been developed over time. I know my neighbourhood well and my face is familiar to lots of people in the area where I live. I have also developed some trusting relationships that have enabled me to share the gospel and pray with some of my neighbours, but these relationships are the product of living in my present house for a decade.

Church planting also takes time, particularly in pioneering situations. Many of today's church plants in the United Kingdom happened when a group of people from a large church began a new church plant in a nearby area. Often, the groups who began these new churches were large enough to start and sustain a full church programme from day one. In much of Europe, this kind of planting is just not possible because there are not enough sufficiently large churches around. More typically, a missionary couple or small mission team will move to a town or area where there are no churches and possibly even no Christians. They are church-planting in pioneer areas and this takes time, often a couple of decades. Missionaries involved in that kind of church planting will need to give years of their life to this ministry.

It is clear that, in order for Europe to be reached, we need both long-term and short-term mission. The long-term missionaries will provide the stability, the abiding relationships, and the required knowledge and experience necessary in mission. Short-term missionaries will provide extra hands and feet, energy, creativity and the pastoral support that will complement the work of long-term missionaries.

Cross-cultural or national worker?

Another aspect is the relative merits of cross-cultural missionaries and national workers (that is, missionaries who work among their own people). Historically speaking, cross-cultural missionaries have been the backbone of the modern missionary movement. Without their endeavour, particular mission fields would never have developed. The reason why cross-cultural missionaries were needed is obvious. Some countries, such as the United Kingdom and the USA, had significant numbers of Christians and churches with a burden for evangelism; so missionaries were sent to countries where the church was either small or barely existed. When GLO first began, the model was cross-cultural mission as the vast majority of our missionaries came from the United Kingdom and went all over Europe with the gospel. This should not surprise us, as the UK had significantly more evangelical Christians than most European countries—in Greece, for example, evangelicals comprise a tiny number. Since those early days, a significant change has taken place. And we can now be active in recruiting national workers.

There is an increasing need to do this, and not just because the spiritual challenges of Europe are so great. For, while evangelicalism in the UK may appear robust, it is also static and could well be in decline, were it not for Christians who immigrate into the UK. Many evangelical congregations in the UK today are predominantly elderly and therefore less likely to be a source of new missionary personnel. And a great many churches in the UK are now more focussed on maintenance and survival, rather than world mission and that needs to be factored in.

There are obvious advantages in using national workers to grow the work of mission. First, as they are working in their own country, they already know the language and culture. There are no visa issues to worry about. Nor will they need to think about going back to their home country for the sake of their children's education, because they already are home. Some cultures within Europe are also extremely hard to break into or are politically volatile; utilising people within such cultures for mission is a significant advantage.

Clearly, utilising national workers is a key issue, and we must consider this in any strategy for the evangelisation of Europe. Of course, first, we need to identify them. This is easier said than done, given that many will come from missionary-receiving countries where evangelicals are few. As an example, I can think of a city in central Europe where I have taken short-term mission teams. That city has a population in excess of 100,000, a medium-sized university, and a teaching hospital, all of which put the city on the map. However, there are only three evangelical churches in the city, the largest of which has a Sunday attendance of around 25 people. It is not hard to imagine that finding a gifted and motivated person there, who is able and willing to engage full-time in mission, will not be easy.

Another challenge is ensuring that those national workers are equipped and trained for the task. The spiritual history of the UK means that it is replete with Bible colleges and there is a whole array of training materials in English that can be used to prepare and equip someone for mission. This is not the case in many parts of Europe, where training institutions and Bible colleges are less numerous, often poorly funded, and struggle to find teaching staff. This raises the question, how do we equip a potential national worker to engage in full-time mission activity in their own country?

One possibility is to bring them to the UK for training. GLO is greatly blessed to have Tilsley College as its training wing, and students have come to the college from all over the world. This works if the person concerned has a good grasp of English (the medium of instruction at Tilsley College); but, if not, it can be impractical. There are other considerations. Is the person married and do they have children? If so, it would be neither practical nor wise for the person to take a year out from family responsibilities to come and study at Tilsley College. The college can and does accommodate families, and this has been done very successfully on occasion. Indeed, the whole family benefits greatly from the experience of living in a different context, and families have often described their time at college as a life-changing experience. This is consequently a very good option and should be the norm. But the practical and financial challenges of doing this, as well as the visa difficulties post-Brexit, should not be underestimated. It is not always possible.

While national workers are a strategic resource, they still need the same care as cross-cultural workers. Most cross-cultural missionaries have a sending church that prays for them regularly and tries to keep in touch. Many churches in the UK also have a culture of financial giving, and prioritise mission in a way that doesn't always happen in other countries. This means that any missionaries that they send out cross-culturally benefit from the mission interest of the church. The majority of cross-cultural missionaries are also linked with a mission organisation that can provide on-the-job training, pastoral care, some financial support, and a range of support services. But that does not mean that cross-cultural missionaries don't have their struggles. On the contrary, it is a challenging calling, but this infrastructure provides a measure of security for them. National workers also need all of this if they are to function effectively, and it may not be present in the particular country. So that needs to be considered as part of any strategic thinking.

Today, mission organisations need to incorporate national workers into their work on equal terms with cross-cultural missionaries, depending on their personal circumstances. This transition has been a great blessing to the work of GLO and we are enriched by having a multicultural GLO mission family.

When it comes to providing support for mission workers, some mission organisations pay a salary, but this is rare. They need to be supported from other sources on a faith basis. Many missionary organisations require the missionary to give a proportion of their income to the mission organisation for administration and management. Often, the proportion can be anything between 10% and 20%. Some also require their missionaries to obtain guarantees of a particular level of support before the mission organisation will allow them to begin their ministry.

In the case of GLO, we are a faith-based ministry and therefore everyone from the General Director to the newest recruit is responsible for his or her own personal finances and trusts God to provide. Nor do we ask our missionaries for any funding to cover our overheads as we, as a whole organisation, live by faith. The challenge that this poses should not be underestimated. Many missionaries rely on their church, other churches, friends, family, as well as some Christian trusts, for their finances. But what happens if you are a national worker, your church is small, the country is poor, your family are not Christians, you are not known by any trusts, and you have very few Christian friends? This is a genuine challenge for many missionaries, but may be especially true of national workers if they do not have well-heeled international connections. It means that mission organisations need to think carefully about the support available and have a sensitive and nuanced response.

A challenge which both cross-cultural missionaries and national workers face is the lack of fellowship. This is particularly the case in a pioneering context where the isolation and loneliness have to be experienced to be truly understood. We have an annual GLO European conference at which we bring together all of our mission partners for a couple of days of Bible teaching, prayer and fellowship. I am always deeply moved to hear our GLO personnel express what being together in that way means to them. One missionary told me that the spiritual food and fellowship that he gets during the annual conference sustains him in his tough ministry for the rest of the year.

As mission organisations, we need to ask, what should our strategy be: using cross-cultural missionaries or national workers? In practice, the answer is likely to be both. The needs are so great that we must find as many people as possible to meet them and that requires using both cross-cultural miss-ionaries and national workers. The context itself will often be a deciding factor. Even in Europe, there are some countries that are fairly inaccessible, have a formidably difficult language, cultural resistance to outsiders, and an education system totally different to that of other European countries. These factors will need to be taken into account when considering who to recruit for the task. In such situations, cross-cultural mission is not impossible, but it would take a particular type of person to engage in mission there. So, finding national workers who are willing to serve God in their own context could be highly strategic.

This joint strategy will be necessary to reach Europe. Mission agencies should be proactive in countries where the church is relatively strong and they should recruit cross-cultural missionaries for areas of Europe where the church is much weaker. They should also work hard in those spiritually needy countries to find Christians who have a heart for God and a desire to reach their fellow citizens with the gospel, and get behind them so that they can be missionaries among their own people. Only by combining both approaches can we hope to make some impact in this needy continent.

Utilising national workers is not just strategic for the countries where they work, but also for those countries where the church is stronger. I know some local churches that have an interest in mission, but do not have anyone from their church who has gone out in mission. Linking a church like this with a national worker is a good way in which they can become actively involved in frontline mission. I also know some Christian businessmen and Christian trusts who have a heart for mission. They too could have an active role in mission work by supporting national workers who may have no other means of support.

Learning lessons

Given these two options for long-term mission, what are the big take-home lessons? First, the days of cross-cultural mission are not over. This kind of mission work has been a staple since the days of the early church and today there are thousands of effective cross-cultural missionaries all over the world. Their very presence in the countries where they serve raises questions, because the people that they are trying to reach are bound to ask what they are doing there. We should never lose sight of the value of cross-cultural mission and there is no better way of involving UK churches in mission than for them to send one of their own to another culture with the good news of Jesus.

Secondly, cross-cultural mission needs to be complemented by the help that can be offered by national workers, with the two working in tandem. The two combined can make a huge impact on the mission field. The needs that confront us in Europe require that we fully exploit both.

Thirdly, we need to find ways of recruiting, training, equipping and supporting national workers. Cross-cultural missionaries need this kind of help, but the challenge is all the greater with respect to national workers. It will mean that mission leaders, as well as cross-cultural missionaries, will need to be talent-spotting people who have the right skill-set and commitment. They will need to find appropriate training pathways to prepare national workers for their ministry. Then comes the need for support. This is a difficult area because, if national workers are totally supported from abroad, the churches in their own country, however small, will never develop a culture of financial giving. We should not just go for short-term gain, but should always look to the future, and work towards a blended approach. That will mean not just finding financial supporters in the UK to help national workers, but sharing the burden across Europe, as well as encouraging the fledgling church in the country that we are working in to take up its responsibility and help support its own home-grown missionaries.

The needs of Europe are great; there is much to be done. Much can be accomplished using all means of missionary activity, but it also needs to be carefully planned and worked out.

What kind of church?

Having thought about what kind of people are needed to reach Europe, we also need to ask what kind of church is likely to survive and even grow in this difficult environment? This is not an academic question. A glance at British church history since the end of World War 2 would show that literally thousands of local churches have declined and closed. Many of their buildings lie empty or are used for other purposes. (Many churches have been planted over the period as well, but the overall balance of numbers is negative.) The UK is a particularly striking example of this, but across Europe many evangelical churches have struggled and continue to do so. If nothing else, this demonstrates that the church in Europe will not automatically grow, so thought needs to be given to what can be done to encourage sustained and sustainable growth of new churches.

This is not an easy question, because there are no silver bullets or methods that guarantee success. However, there are things that will definitely help.

The first thing is **unity**. Divided churches do not grow, because they are too busy infighting, firefighting, or just trying, often fruitlessly, to keep everyone happy. Working hard at unity is a key feature.

If churches are unified, they can focus on the crucial issue of **evangelism**—reaching out to their local community. There is a huge temptation, especially in a small church, to become inward-focussed, caring only for existing members. This may be an understandable reaction, but in the long run it will be detrimental. Of course, churches need to care for their own, because the church is a family. But churches need to be determined to reach out as well, to welcome the stranger, and to ensure that sharing the gospel is a high priority. Evangelism is costly in the effort required, and shaping the church to reach out will mean that church members cannot just become comfortable in their own 'holy huddle'. It takes determination and courage to keep evangelism at the forefront, but, when churches do that, they also discover that engaging in evangelism keeps them sharp, and encourages and grows their faith. In particular, churches should prioritise personal evangelism, so that each member of the church is active in sharing their faith with people round about them. A church whose members are mobilised to share the gospel in everyday life will be more effective than one which merely relies on good church-based programmes. It will reach far more people, because there will be many, especially in a European context, who would not attend an evangelistic event or begin attending a church, but they can be reached through personal friendships.

Another important requirement is **flexibility**. Churches can very easily get into a rut, going through the motions, doing things just because they have always been done that way. A church that is not willing to embrace change will probably not last, especially when culture is constantly and quickly evolving. Churches need flexibility, so that they can respond to changing circumstances and, if something does not work, they need to be willing to try something else.

Added to this, churches need to be **relational**. The local church should not be an institution, but rather a family. Getting together cannot just be about having a programme of meetings. Rather, the church is a community that does life together and bases its life on the quality of its relationships.

Finally, churches need to remember the importance of **discipleship**. Jesus spent quality time with his disciples, pouring his life into them. Having developed them as people in this way, he was able to release them, so that they too could make disciples. Churches will grow best if there is intentional discipleship that produces good fruit in the life their members.

We repeat, there are no silver bullets. Evangelism is hard, mission is challenging, and Europe has monumental spiritual needs. However, if we think and plan carefully and do the right things, many more people in Europe will be challenged with the claims of Christ, and Europe may experience another spiritual harvest.

In the next chapter, we will be looking at an important question for anyone interested in mission. Europe is a big place, and mission personnel and resources are always limited. It is therefore important to ask what are the key mission priorities. We want to propose some priorities for consideration by mission service groups, supporting churches, potential missionaries, and anyone prayerfully interested in mission.

Chapter 9

Mission priorities

I love walking through a mature forest. There is something majestic and awe-inspiring about trees. They are strong, often tall, and many of the trees you see in a mature forest have lived much longer than you have! However, there is something else that you realise when you walk through a forest: you are only aware of what is directly around you. You cannot see the edges of the forest, and so you have no real idea of where you are in it or of how big the forest is.

Sometimes being in mission can feel a bit like this. Missionaries can be involved in their small corner, dealing with the immediate and with the people whom they are currently caring for. This, of course, is a good thing, but, by being so absorbed in the present, they can lose sight of the big picture and the strategic needs that should be addressed.

One of the great challenges that we face as we reflect on the spiritual needs of Europe and the demands of the Great Commission is, what are some of the strategic areas of work that we need to keep our eyes on? The list of strategic priorities is extensive, but we will focus on the main ones.

Unreached Europe

At the top of the list must be the unreached parts of Europe. While wider Europe as a whole is needy, the difference between the most spiritually needy parts and the others is stark. This can be illustrated by comparing four different countries: the UK where evangelicals, Pentecostals and Charismatics together account for somewhere between 8% and 15% of the population, the Netherlands where they are 4%, France where they are 2%, and Greece,

Bosnia and Herzegovina, and North Macedonia where they account only for 1% of the population.[1]

It should go without saying that, if we want to be really strategic in mission, we need to give particular focus to those areas where there are the fewest committed Christians. That will involve doing two things. First, when we look at countries as a whole, we should ask whether there are areas within the country that require pioneer missionary work. This is important because, even in countries where there has been growth and a lot of active missionary work, there can still be areas and people groups that are unreached. In France for example, while Bible-based Christianity is growing and there is an increasing number of vibrant churches, there are still 35,000 'communes' (the lowest governmental area ranging from rural villages to cities) with no vibrant church. Likewise in Italy, there are vibrant and active churches especially in the south, and evangelicals etc. are about 3% of the population. However, there are large sections of the country where Bible-based Christianity has hardly penetrated. Indeed, 70% of Italy's 8000 plus 'comuni' (governmental areas as in France) have no evangelical, Pentecostal or Charismatic church. The island of Sardinia is an example of this where there are only around 30 such churches among the 1.67 million islanders.

Secondly, we should ask if there are any concentrations of countries where there are few evangelicals? In Europe, this immediately points us to areas such as the Balkans. In this group of ten countries, nine are countries where evangelicals comprise less than 0.6% of population and four of them have only one evangelical Christian for every 1,000 people, which is less than even countries like Saudi Arabia or Iraq (though the approach of these Muslim states is to tolerate churches of expatriate believers so long as they do not proselytise among the indigenous Muslim population). Once again, if we are serious about strategically evangelising Europe, we need to give a real focus to areas like the Balkans.

Immigration

Another strategic area of work is among immigrant communities. The reality is that people from all over the world are coming to Europe, many legally, some

---

1. The figures are those given in *World Christian Enclyclopedia* for 2020 (see appendix E) except for the UK where the range of figures suggested by *World Christian Encyclopedia* and *Operation World* is given.

illegally. Of course, immigration has always been a feature of European life, but this has been particularly marked since World War 2, especially in western Europe. As a result, many European countries have a significant proportion of their population whose parents or one parent is foreign born. These include Switzerland with 47%, Sweden 31%, Austria 30%, France 27%, Belgium 25%, Germany 24% and the UK 23%.[2] Quite apart from the significant change that this must create in the ethnic mix of those countries, it stands to reason that this is also a significant mission issue. It means that when working in any of these countries, missionaries, evangelists and churches will need to be aware of the great diversity within the societies that they are trying to reach and will need to adapt to the many different communities that now inhabit today's Europe. We should note that, while immigrants to an unfamiliar culture sometimes take comfort from the religion in which they were brought up, other immigrants are often willing to revaluate their thinking, even on matters as fundamental as the religion that they were born into. So they can be a fruitful field for evangelism.

It also means that the needs of Europe grow ever larger. Fifty years ago, the population of Europe was a little over 672 million; today it is over 742 million, an increase of 70 million.[3] Insofar as this increase is attributable to immigration, some have been Christians and have brought an increased spiritual vitality to many parts of Europe. Many more have been from other religious groupings and have increased the spiritual challenges of Europe.

Islam

The growth of Islam in Europe is of particular note, as it is now the second largest religion after Christianity. While Muslims comprised only 2% of Europe's population in 1950, by 2020 they accounted for 6% and the proportion is still growing.[4] This is the result not only of immigration, but also because of higher birthrates among Islamic communities, while birthrates among indigenous Europeans scarcely achieve replacement.

---

2. Financial Times, 'Right wing presidential candidates immigration obsession belies reality of modern France', 26.9.2023.

3. https://www.macrotrends.net/countries/eur/europe/population

4. International Journal of Environmental Science and Development, Vol. 1, No. 2, June 2010, p. 154.

■ 90–100%   Azerbaijan, Kosovo, Turkey
■ 70–90%   Albania, Kazakhstan
■ 50–70%   Bosnia and Herzegovina
▦ 30–40%   North Macedonia
▦ 10–20%   Bulgaria, Cyprus, Georgia, Montenegro, Russia
▦ 5–10%   Austria, Sweden, Belgium, France, Germany, Greece, Liechtenstein,
            Netherlands, Switzerland, United Kingdom, Norway, Denmark
  4–5%   Italy, Serbia
  2–4%   Luxembourg, Malta, Slovenia, Spain
  1–2%   Croatia, Ireland, Ukraine
▢ < 1%   Andorra, Armenia, Belarus, Czech Republic, Estonia, Finland, Hungary, Iceland, Latvia,
            Lithuania, Moldova, Monaco, Poland, Portugal, Romania, San Marino, Slovakia

Islam in Europe

This presents a great opportunity, as well as a considerable challenge. The upside is that a great many of Europe's Muslims are deeply moral people who espouse family values and are a buffer against the increasing secularisation of European culture. Many are spiritually attuned and willing to discuss matters of faith, which means they are open to Christians sharing the gospel with them.

The fact that they live in Europe means they can be evangelised in safety, and their extended relationships mean that they could be a channel for reaching Muslims in very closed countries. This point was impressed on me when I was leading a short-term mission team at the Birmingham Commonwealth Games in 2022. We were doing street work and passing out gospel portions. I had the opportunity for conversation with a young mother named Halloumi. She had been born in Somalia, and her parents then became guest workers in Saudi Arabia. After returning to Somalia, she married, and then she and her husband fled the country and were living in Norway. She was in Birmingham for a few weeks, to visit family there. As I shared the gospel with her, the thought struck me that if she became a Christian, she would have ongoing contact with Muslim friends and family members in Saudi Arabia and Somalia, as well as different parts of Europe, so her conversion would be truly strategic.

As well as the opportunities, however, there are also major challenges. In many European countries, Muslims have not assimilated well into their community and tend to live together in areas of high Muslim population, where they are less easy to reach, despite the freedom to do so in principle. Islam is a missionary religion like Christianity, and thousands of indigenous Europeans convert to Islam every year, often women who have married Muslim men.

From a mission point of view, it is clear that reaching Muslims in Europe is a significant strategic priority.

Student population

Another strategic priority is to reach university students. Among today's students are tomorrow's doctors, teachers, politicians, media leaders and social influencers. They will be the people who build and shape the future. University is a crucial time in which lives are shaped. Many Christians who go to university discover that it can be a make-or-break time for them spiritually. This is because at university they are exposed to a whole range of different and competing viewpoints and are taught to think and to analyse. This same thought-provoking environment opens up great opportunities for evangelism. Students are often ready to change their minds about fundamental matters. Many students, too, are from the Majority World and likely to return to their home countries, so in that way too they are strategic for Christian outreach.

The sheer size of Europe's student population is staggering. At any one time, it numbers in the millions. For example, Italy has a student population of 1.85 million spread across 94 universities. GBU (Gruppi Biblici Universitari—part of IFES) has only around 30 groups gathering around 300 students in total. Milan alone has 175,000 students, among whom very little evangelism is being done. Parachurch organisations have an important role to play in reaching Europe's student population, but so too do local churches as they can offer a spiritual home to students.

Big cities

Another strategic mission field within Europe is the big cities. It is often the case that churches and Christians have vacated the heart of Europe's urban centres, to live somewhere less pressurised. But there is a strategic need to make inroads back into Europe's great cities. They tend to be multicultural, vibrant and influential. A good example is Brussels, a city of 1.1 million people where 32% of the city are non-Belgian, 13% Muslim, and there are 45 nationalities of 1,000 people or more: Brussels is a true melting pot. It also has an increasing number of impoverished neighbourhoods, as well as many affluent young professionals. Another example is London where the Office of National Statisitics reports that the city comprises of 43.4% white British, 14.6% non-British white, 20.8% Asian, and 7.9% black African, while 25% of the population claimed a religious affiliation other than Christianity.[5] In the 2021 Census, 37% of Londoners declared themselves to have been foreign-born. To evangelise London is to evangelise the world.

Cities, particularly big cities, are exciting places to live, but not always easy places to live. They are crowded, expensive, fast-paced, often impersonal and, given that they are a melting pot, it takes a particular mindset to fit in. They are, however, key places for mission and so must remain a strategic priority.

---

5 https://www.ons.gov.uk/peoplepopulationandcommunity/populationandmigration/ populationestimates/articles/populationestimatesbyethnicgroupandreligionenglandandwales/ 2019#:~:text=London%20was%20the%20most%20ethnically,an%20estimated%20 10.6%25%20of%20the

Minority communities

A final area that should be considered strategic are minority communities. These communities are often overlooked by wider culture, as well as by governments, and often experience prejudice and hardship. Europe's largest ethnic minority are the Roma or Gypsies, who number some 12 million, of whom 6 million reside within the EU.[6] Roma is an umbrella-term, which covers diverse groups such as the Yenish, Romanichels, Travellers, Ashkali and Boyash. In many parts of Europe, and especially central and Eastern Europe, the Roma face a great deal of discrimination. Indeed, research from the European Commission suggests that only 39% of European citizens think that they would feel comfortable if their children had Roma classmates and only 2% of Roma attend post-secondary education.

Evangelism among Roma peoples is often made difficult because of their social isolation and suspicion, sometimes provoked by their treatment at the hands of the wider population. Many Roma communities are poor, less well-educated, and have a reputation for criminality. Given the sheer number of Roma and their widespread distribution across Europe, they should certainly be considered a strategic priority. In many places, evangelism among the Roma has proved very fruitful, on occasion to the extent of revival, and this has demonstrated that these communities can be reached.

What kind of ministry?

As we think of these major areas of need, we also have to think strategically about the kind of ministries that will be needed and effective in Europe in the immediate future. We reflect on just a few.

Church planting

First and foremost, Europe needs church planting. Given that so many areas of Europe have no evangelical church, it is not hard to see why this must be a priority. Not only does church planting bring Christian witness into an area,

---

6. https://commission.europa.eu/strategy-and-policy/policies/justice-and-fundamental-rights/combatting-discrimination/roma-eu/roma-equality-inclusion-and-participation-eu_en#:~:text=The%20Roma%20are%20Europe's%20largest,ban%20across%20EU%20Member%20States.

it is also a very effective form of evangelism. This is because when someone is involved in a church plant, their whole focus is on making contact with people who are not Christians and sharing the gospel with them. No church plant can take off without a focus on intentional evangelism and a commitment to using every opportunity to share the good news of Jesus. It is this intentionality that makes church plants an effective evangelistic tool.

Church planting can also be shaped to be relevant and effective in a given area. One of the challenges that some established churches face is that they can become tradition-bound and inflexible. Of course, this is not inevitable, but it does happen and as a result they are resistant to change. Church planters, on the other hand, are starting from scratch and have the freedom to contextualise what they are doing to make it relevant for their particular area.

Many Christians, even missionaries, fear being involved in a church plant as it seems so daunting. It is, of course, challenging to plant the church and it takes a great deal of effort; but it is also difficult to maintain an existing church, particularly if the church has problems that are difficult to solve. Neither church planting nor church leadership is for the faint hearted, but nor are they impossible, even in a place like Europe. With hard work, commitment and lots of prayer, churches can be planted even in the most difficult of areas.[7]

Evangelism

Closely linked to church planting is evangelism, which is also much needed. This is at the very heart of the missionary endeavour and is particularly relevant to Europe. If we were to look at another part of the world, say, for example, sub-Saharan Africa, it would not make much sense to send significant numbers of cross-cultural missionaries there to do evangelism, because not only is the evangelical community there already large and vibrant, but Christians are already highly successful in sharing the gospel. The same cannot be said for large swathes of Europe. Many evangelical churches are small and struggling, and lack confidence. In countries that were formerly behind the Iron Curtain, some churches still struggle with the legacy of communism and all the

---

7. On church planting, see Stephen McQuoid & Neil Summerton (ed's), *Fresh Shoots in Stony Ground: The challenges of church planting* (Portishead and Tiverton, UK: Church Planting Initiative & Partnership, 2012).

restrictions that they suffered. As a result, they are hesitant when it comes to evangelism and are not sure even how to begin. Having a missionary or national worker serving alongside them in evangelism can be an enormous help and highly strategic.

Short-term mission

Short-term mission should also be on the agenda. Since the end of World War 2, it has grown in prominence and has become a significant feature of mission life. However, in recent years, short-term mission has had to face some challenges. First, the global pandemic brought all short-term mission to a halt and getting things started again has proved challenging. Secondly, some people have begun to question the environmental impact of the travel involved. More worryingly, there is a reaction, particularly from some younger evangelicals, to any form of confrontational evangelism or evangelistic methods that involve more that sharing the gospel through friendship. This has had its effect on short-term mission, which often utilises forms of evangelism, such as street theatre and open-air preaching that seem overt and confrontational.

Despite these obstacles, short-term mission should still be considered strategic for several reasons. First, done well, it can still be used very effectively in evangelism. Secondly, it can be very encouraging, particularly for small churches, to receive teams of enthusiastic Christians who work with them for a week or two and assist in the church's outreach. Thirdly, the extra hands and feet that a short-term mission team provides can achieve a great deal in a short period of time. Finally, short-term mission is a good way of discipling people, strengthening their own faith, and giving them an insight into the world of mission. It is significant that many of the career missionaries serving with GLO first became interested in mission, and in their country of service, through short-term mission. It is therefore something to which we must continue to commit ourselves.

Training and upskilling

Another strategic ministry is training which can take place in various ways. At GLO, we have our own Bible college, Tilsley College, which offers re-sidential training programmes for up to three years. However, we also offer church-based training and that has proved to be highly strategic in mission. Church-based training has the benefit of being flexible, mobile, and does not rely on much infrastructure.

Training can also be delivered in a wide variety of ways. A church building, or any public accommodation, can be used for night classes which can provide vocational and theological training for church leaders and members. Day seminars and workshops can also be offered, and these can tackle specific issues or be aimed at upskilling people, so that they work more efficiently in their ministries. Another form of training is mentoring an individual, or a group, over a period of time. Part of my ministry is to meet one-on-one with a number of young church leaders, so as to mentor them in their role. The reason why church-based training is so strategic in the mission field is twofold. First, we will never find enough cross-cultural missionaries to meet all the needs on the mission field, so we need to equip local Christians. Secondly, there are key people already in place in mission situations all over Europe and equipping them to be better at what they do adds huge value to what is already taking place in those locations. In that sense, training itself is mission.

Caring ministries

Among all the other priorities, we should never forget caring ministries. This is perhaps a less obvious need given the relative prosperity of Europe. However, three things should be considered. First, Scripture urges us to express the love of Christ in tangible ways. Secondly, there is real value in viewing mission holistically. And thirdly, there are real social needs in Europe. There is poverty, which is why so many food banks have sprung up; deprivation is real, and social concern can be expressed in positive ways as a companion of gospel proclamation. Moreover, Europe has so many social problems, including significant addiction issues, as well as dysfunctional families and communities, that there is a huge need for caring ministries.

There has always been a debate in the mission community about the balance between evangelism and social concern. It could be argued that the greatest need in Europe is for people to receive the gospel, which in itself would meet many social needs as lives are transformed. However, it can also be argued that showing practical care is part of our sharing the good news about Jesus, as his own teaching, miracles, and compassion show. Demonstrating Christ's love in action is a powerful way of opening people up to the importance of personal faith in Christ.

As we maintain caring ministries as a strategic part of our missionary enterprise in Europe, we also give a role to missionaries and national workers who may not be gifted specifically in evangelism, but can make an important contribution to mission by feeding the hungry, loving the outcast and the marginalised, and demonstrating the practical love of Christ in action.

Resources (including online)

A final strategic ministry is that of producing resources for mission. This is a vital but often unsung ministry. Resources of all sorts are needed if Europe is to be reached for Christ. We need gospel tracts, Bible translations, discipleship programmes, resources for children and young people, theological books and study aids, Bible commentaries and Sunday school materials, websites, apps and whatever will become available in the future through AI. The truth is that the list is endless, but it can all make a huge contribution to the work of mission.

Chapter 9

Your choice

By now, you should have a good idea of the kind of place Europe is and just how difficult it is to evangelise. We also hope that you are starting to develop a real burden for the spiritual needs of Europe, as well as a desire to do something about them. Getting involved in the great task of evangelising Europe does not necessarily involve going there as a missionary, though that may be an outcome. But it should involve taking some kind of responsibility, showing some interest, and taking active steps to engage with all that God is doing throughout wider Europe. If that is what you are prepared and challenged to do, here are some of the steps that can draw you into God's plans for the evangelisation of Europe.

Be informed

The first thing that you can do is to inform yourself about what is happening across Europe. This is important, because the more you know about a place, the greater your interest in it is likely to be. This will involve keeping your eyes and ears open and being deliberately alert to Europe and its needs.

Doing this is fairly simple. Whenever any European country features on the news, pay attention! If you see a newspaper or magazine article on Europe, take the time to read it. Read books like this one, or any book that can inform you about life across Europe and what is happening. There are also books, websites and apps that provide information about the spiritual needs of Europe, so you can familiarise yourself with some of these. Even going on holiday to any European country, and being observant about what you see, will be of help. My wife and I did a city break in Paris a few years ago and we left with two overwhelming impressions. First, we were struck by the fact that the area in which we were staying was overwhelmingly Muslim, with many of the women wearing traditional Islamic dress. The other was a simple observation that, while we walked for miles up and down a large number of streets, we did not come across a single evangelical church. Both these impressions have stayed with us ever since.

Pray

Not only could you be learning more about Europe; you could be praying for Europe. Praying regularly for something is difficult unless you have specific things to pray about. It is here that your growing knowledge about Europe will come in useful, as it will provide fuel for prayer. It is also helpful to get in touch with mission organisations and missionaries who are working in Europe. They will be happy to provide you with information on spiritual needs and prayer letters and publications that give helpful information. GLO has a magazine, *e-vision*, which informs readers about our activities in Europe.

It is also useful to attend mission events and conferences where you not only learn more about what is going on in Europe, but you can also meet other people who have an interest in mission. These events are good places to connect with mission organisations and get to know more about how they work. There is particular value in getting to know missionaries serving in Europe and keeping in touch with them. They will value your friendship, and you can inform your prayer life through that friendship.

Get involved

Your quest does not need to stop at the 'getting information' stage, or even the praying stage. There are more ways than ever of getting personally involved in mission. One great way of doing this is to take part in a short-term mission team. Every year GLO runs mission teams which last from a few days to two weeks. The range of activities on these teams is enormous. Many distribute literature; some do open-air work, coffee mornings and community events. Some teams focus on English conversation classes, while others do children's work or youth work. Whatever the activity, they are designed to get the gospel across to people. Discipleship is also a important part of short-term mission, which is why every GLO team includes Bible teaching and times of prayer together. Short-term mission teams are an excellent way of getting to know a European country. They also give team members some sense of what mission involves. A great many long-term GLO missionaries began their mission interest by going on a short-term team. You may already have an interest in a European country, in which case you could also consider helping to recruit for and lead a short-term mission team.

There are other ways of getting involved in mission. Often, there are specific projects that need to be done, for example building work or logistics. Those who manage these projects are always looking for volunteers who are willing to give time and energy to them. There are many teaching and training opportunities. GLO is particularly involved in central and Eastern Europe by offering training to church leaders, evangelists and other church members. If you have ability in lecturing and experience in church leadership or Bible teaching, this is a great way to get involved.

Give

Another positive way of getting involved in mission is to provide for it financially. This is a very practical thing to do, because mission does need to be financed, and mission activity in Europe is more expensive than in other parts of the world because Europe is an expensive place. Moreover, because Europe is such a spiritually hard place, progress is often slow. While the one-off gift or legacy will meet an immediate need, financial support for mission in Europe also requires long-term commitment, in which faithful supporters get behind missionaries and mission activity and enable them through sacrificial giving over the long haul.

Sometimes those who give are busy business-people or professionals, and they cannot offer much of their valuable time to the cause of mission. However, their generosity in giving makes mission possible. Experience has also taught me that many who give are not wealthy, but their real commitment is demonstrated through sacrificial giving. Mission would not be possible without the willingness of Christians to give, and their ministry of giving should be recognised as a bedrock of missionary enterprise.

Be a mission champion

It is also very beneficial to have mission champions in local churches. A mission champion is simply someone who promotes the cause of mission in their own church and among their circle of influence. There are many ways of doing this. One mission champion connected to GLO promotes short-term mission teams in his church and also recruits people for teams as well as leading them. Other mission champions ensure that GLO literature is always available in their churches and that mission events and activities are always profiled within the life of the church.

Another mission champion organises a mission prayer meeting in her home. She invites Christians, whether from her church or others, and motivates them to pray. She also invites missionaries to attend when they are on home assignment so that they can connect with the people who are praying for them. Most mission champions will never become missionaries themselves. However, what they do for the cause of mission is invaluable. They keep mission on the agenda in their local church and raise a great deal of prayer support. They also keep people informed about what is happening in mission. Very often mission champions develop strong friendships with missionaries and their friendship is greatly valued.

Train and go

For some people, simply being involved incrementally in mission is not enough. They feel so burdened about mission, often a specific mission location, that they feel compelled to give up their job and become a missionary full-time. This is a huge step, but an important one, because there is no substitute for someone giving their life for the cause of mission. It is through career missionaries that churches get planted and mission becomes thoroughly established in countries.

This is a big step and it cannot be taken casually. Those committing their lives to mission need to think carefully, not only about the kind of work they will be doing in mission, but also about the challenges of living in a new country or area. This can be particularly demanding if it involves families. Missionaries with families need to think about their children's education and the possibility that those children will be away from family and friends for prolonged periods of time. In Europe, where the standard of education is good, the fact that children are brought up and educated in the country may mean that they identify with that country and remain when their parents retire to their home country: their children may be French, for example, while they remain British or German. This is not a negligible matter.

A missionary career is a momentous life choice, which needs to be a response to a genuine call from God. Nevertheless, it is highly recommended that anyone making such a step should undertake personal preparation and training. At GLO, we have seen over many years the benefits of good preparation, and that is the reason for the existence of Tilsley College. The college helps candidates prepare for a life in mission by offering courses that teach not only biblical studies and theology, but also provide skills training and development in discipleship and spiritual disciplines. Those who teach are practitioners, and the whole college is unashamedly focussed on mission. We strongly recommend that anyone hoping to go full-time into mission spends at least one year studying at Tilsley College in preparation.

Where now?

Each of these are ways of getting involved in mission, and they are all valuable. Most people reading this book will not become full-time missionaries; however, in order for mission to happen at all, we all have a role to play. At the sharp end, there are people who are called to give up their jobs, or their current work for the Lord, and go to a mission location to serve him. But for every person who does this, there needs to be dozens of others who stay behind and become part of the support services for mission. All are needed and our hope is that, having read this book, you will take an interest in mission in Europe and be determined to play your part in response to the Lord's leading.

Appendix A

Types of mission in Europe today

Examples of ministry in Europe

Europe is a large, diverse and complex place. The needs are enormous and so are the opportunities. There is no 'one-size-fits-all' type of missionary or mission activity. In this appendix, we look briefly at some of the different types of mission work that are being done, by focussing in on the ministry of some present-day missionaries and mission situations. Most are linked with GLO, but not all.

Philippe and Marie-Christine Perrilliat

Philippe and Marie-Christine are seasoned missionaries (in this case, national workers) who have been involved in various church plants for over thirty years. More recently, they have been applying their experience in a new project in the university city of Aix-en-Provence, France. The project is multifaceted. It is a church plant, as the spiritual needs of the city are immense. In the building which is the church's base, they have also opened a coffee shop so that they can attract students from the nearby university and this is the basis of a vibrant student ministry. Additionally, the project trains church planters. Prospective church planters come and work with them in Aix, normally for a period of two years. After this, the trainees go elsewhere to plant their own church. Philippe also lectures in the Geneva Bible School, where he can recruit church planters. He is also involved in mentoring the leaders of other churches to help them grow. Philippe and Marie-Christine are a good example of an experienced missionary couple who have adapted their ministry for greater impact.

Cristi and Simona Sortan

Cristi and Simona Sortan are members of a new generation of missionaries with GLO. They work in their own country of Romania. Cristi's father and mother are also GLO missionaries and, as national workers, have been instrumental in planting a number of new churches among Gypsy communities in Romania. Cristi trained at Tilsley College and then returned to work in those Gypsy communities. His focus is working with young people, both in evangelism and discipling young Christians. As family responsibility permits, Simona will also become more involved in the ministry. They hold regular Bible studies, organize trips and camps, and serve in practical ways. This ministry is the more challenging because the Gypsy communities are a despised minority on the edge of Romanian society, and their education and life opportunities are lower than those of other Romanian young people.

Regin and Heidi Guttesen

Regin and Heidi Guttesen are cross-cultural missionaries in Italy. Regin is Faroese and Heidi is half-American, half-Faroese, and grew up in the Philippines. They served for a number of years in Naples before moving to a much more rural area to help plant a church in Pietracella. Rural Italy has huge church planting needs, as there are literally thousands of towns and villages without an evangelical church. Their church comprises both Italians and immigrants. Regin is a musician, and writes and records worship songs which are widely used by evangelicals in Italy. In addition, they run an annual short-term mission and Bible school in Italy for Faroese young people.

Robert and Emese Lemperger

Robert and Emese live in the university town of Eger in Hungary. They help to lead a small evangelical church, and host short-term mission teams to Hungary. They also run a Christian publishing ministry in which they translate and publish in Hungarian significant theological books; this ministry serves the church in Hungary and Hungarian-speaking churches elsewhere in central Europe. The publishing ministry also produces an evangelical magazine aimed at motivating, educating and encouraging Hungarian-speaking Christians across Europe. They also support a wide range of evangelistic outreaches by providing free gospel literature and books. These go into prisons, nurseries and schools, among other places.

Mayeul and Eva Aureille

Mayeul and Eva along with their three children live in Marseilles, France. They took a sabbatical in the UK, to train at Tilsley College and also travel around the country, visiting churches and learning more about church work. They returned to Marseilles as GLO missionaries, to get involved in church ministry. Mayeul is an elder in a church that was planted by GLO missionaries and he supervises two projects from that church. One is a café ministry in the very centre of the city; the other is a missional community in the satellite town of Aubagne. The café ministry 'Bulle 2 Café' is run by around 30 church volunteers and hosts Bible studies, social events, student groups, and youth work.

Chris and Michelle Hall

Chris and Michelle and their two children live in Chateau-Gontier, a town in one of the most spiritually deprived regions in France. They share their faith through a range of musical activities in church settings, as well as in restaurants and bars. They also run a community choir that gives performances and enables them to spend time sharing life with the choir members. This in turn opens up opportunities for gospel witness. This is complemented by English-language activities, and writing and publishing poetry. They lead and organise various music and English-language workshops for young and old.

Richard and Pam Harknett

Richard and Pam live in Bishop's Stortford, a commuter town just north of London. Having served as missionaries with GLO in Peru for just over a decade, they returned to the UK to develop a training and equipping ministry. Richard is engaged in Bible teaching through 'Joshua', a church-based leadership programme, and through teaching and training in local churches. He also does training in the Hispanic world and in Eastern Europe (in the latter case supporting the work of the Philadelphia Trust). Pam does schools' work in Bishop's Stortford and Harlow, an area with 30 primary schools. She is part of a team that does school assemblies, puppetry and special children's events. Richard and Pam are also heavily involved in ministries in their own church.

Ermal and Denisa Bimaj

Ermal and Denisa Bimaj and their two boys and twin girls live in the Albanian city of Vlore. Following study at Tilsley College, they returned to Albania as GLO missionaries where, as national workers, they work together with colleagues, Juli and Ela Muhameti. They serve in a youth ministry called 'Living Stones', as well as with 'Josiah Venture' in Albania. The aim of Ermal and Denisa is to see young people in Albania come to Christ and give their lives to him. They then disciple these young people and offer mentoring guidance for the future.

Appendix B

My next steps in mission

This book may be encouraging you to to commit your life to the cause of mission. There is no one pathway to doing this. Everyone's pathway is different, as is what they do in mission. However, there are some basic steps that you could take to move forward from where you are now.

1. You need prayerfully to ask yourself what kind of contribution you want to make in mission and ask where God is leading and guiding you. There is need everywhere and so these questions are important. For example, would you think of being a cross-cultural missionary or would you prefer to remain and serve where you are? Are you gifted or burdened to work on the front line, doing something like church planting; or are you more equipped for working behind the scenes? Mission organisations like GLO Europe need both. We need front-line evangelists and church planters, as well as people who can work in administration, teach in our college, cook for the students, or be involved in mission mobilising around the churches. You should also think about whether you want to be involved in mission full-time, or continue in secular employment and do what you can in your available time.

2. Once you begin to get clarity as to how you think the Lord is calling you to mission, it is important to discuss the matter with your church leaders. This is not just to get their advice and prayers, but because, if you are going to commit yourself to mission, you will need your church to be behind you. Keeping in touch with your church

leaders, and engaging them at an early stage in the process, will prove incredibly beneficial in the long run.

3. You will also need to have some detailed conversations with the leaders of GLO Europe or whatever organisation you are thinking of working with. Each organisation will have its own application and orientation process. Some training may also be necessary. In GLO Europe, people generally need to do at least the one-year certificate course at Tilsley College before joining GLO.

4. Before you begin, it is also important both to learn more about the ministry that you will be doing and to get to know the people that you will be working with. For example, if you are joining a church-planting team somewhere in Europe (including in the UK), you should organise visits there beforehand, so that when you finally arrive, you will be familiar with the location. There are also practicalities, such as finding somewhere to live, finding schools for your children (if you have any), opening a bank account, etc.

5. Raising prayer and financial support are also very important, especially if you will be giving up a job to engage full-time in ministry. Again, there is no one way of doing this. Word of mouth is one way; you should talk to as many Christian friends as you think may be interested in your future ministry. It can also be a great help to produce a regular prayer letter, to keep people informed about what you will be doing. Your own church leaders will be able to advise you on some of these matters.

6. Last but not least, there is spiritual preparation. Giving your life to mission is a momentous thing and you will need to call upon all the spiritual resources at your disposal. It is essential, therefore, that you live in a close relationship with Christ, listening to his voice, growing spiritually, and asking God for help to be obedient to his commands on a daily basis.

Appendix C

GLO Europe:
its history and ministry today

GLO Europe

The work of GLO began in Australia in 1965 when a passionate and visionary young Christian, Colin Tilsley, began to mobilise teams of people to go to strategic cities to engage in widespread evangelism. The very first team consisted of 10 members who went to the city of Madras for two years and managed to sell half a million gospel packages.

Following the success of that venture, Colin continued to mobilise Christians all over Australia, as well as establishing a training centre where they could be equipped for missionary activity. Once the work had gained momentum in Australia, he moved to New Zealand in 1967 to repeat the process, before coming to the UK in 1971 where he began to establish the work of GLO in Europe.

Today GLO is an international network comprising several independent branches with hundreds of members and operating in countries all over the world. GLO Europe, which operates from Motherwell in Scotland, is a pan-European work, focussing on evangelism, church planting, training, and resourcing mission.

Why Europe?

Europe is one of the most spiritually needy places on earth and the only continent in the world where the church has shrunk over the past 50 years. Some of the most unreached areas of the world are to be found in Europe, and the population of Europe has grown by 70 million since 1950. Islam is on the rise and the overall number of Muslims in Europe has grown from 19 million to over 44 million over the past 50 years. Meanwhile, Europe is also becoming more secular and liberal.

Globally Christianity is on the rise and there is a real sense in which Europe is being left behind. This list showing evangelical Christians in different parts of the world, powerfully illustrates the point:

Europe 18 million
Africa 182 million
Americas 94 million
Asia 146 million

What is GLO Europe?

GLO Europe is a mission family whose purpose is '*growing mission focused churches in Europe*'. Our desire is to mobilise and motivate Christians all over Europe to share the good news about Jesus, so that the church can become strong and vibrant and replicate itself everywhere in wider Europe.

How do we achieve this?

Four words sum up what the GLO strategy for Europe is all about:

EVANGELISE—we want to reach as many people as possible with the gospel of Jesus Christ, using every appropriate method.

ESTABLISH—we want to plant local churches, and strengthen existing ones, so as to extend God's kingdom.

TRAIN—we want to equip Christians to be more effective in sharing their faith and serving their community, as well as in leading effectively in the church.

RESOURCE—we want to resource mission all over Europe and provide Christians with the tools for effective service.

GLO Europe is a faith-based work. We do not salary our mission personnel, but all of us, whether in front-line mission or working behind the scenes in support services, trust God for our personal finances. We also work in partnership with local churches.

As a mission family, we believe that mission strategy should be developed on the ground and that everyone can have a sense of ownership of the vision. We are a multicultural family, united by our desire to bring the good news of Jesus to Europe.

GLO has several key features that help us in achieving our goals.

First, there is *Tilsley College*, our training wing which provides a range of courses to equip Christians to serve their church and community. This is coupled with a wide range of church-based training options that we also offer.

Secondly, *The GLO Centre* is our base in Motherwell and includes a Christian bookshop, a coffee shop and conference facilities, as well as Tilsley College. The centre is committed not just to serving mission needs in Europe, but also serving the local community, and an independent local church uses the centre.

The GLO Bookshop is Scotland's leading independent Christian bookshop, stocks more than 20,000 items, and draws customers from all over central Scotland and beyond. We have facilities for internet, phone and email sales, and the GLO Bookshop regularly sends books and other resources all over the world.

The Coffee Shop provides a meeting place for the local community in a warm Christian atmosphere. There is no such thing as a typical customer. Some are Christians, many are not. Some customers come with a purpose. For example, pastors meet members of their congregation, business people meet clients, or care workers meet with the people whom they support. Most, however, are friends meeting up over food or a drink. The Coffee Shop also serves the groups that use our conference facilities. These facilities comprise rooms ranging from a 10-seater board room to a 250-seater auditorium.

GLO Media offers practical help to churches and Christian organisations. We have developed skill in communications and filmmaking, and we want to share these resources with others. We offer filming, video editing, and media advice. We can also set up the infrastructure for live broadcasting, and can produce everything from music and promotional videos to full documentaries. All of this can help a church or Christian organisation spread its message and become better known.

GLO Publishing is an expanding service. It now publishes the periodical, *Perspectives*, twice a year, a publication which aims in particular to help local church leaderships in their task. We also produce books and booklets that are of help to local churches and local church leaders. These cover subjects like evangelism, mission, discipleship, leadership, pastoral care, youth and children's work, and church growth.

Preparing to defend the faith: useful books

There are a great many books on the subject of apologetics. It is difficult to know what to exclude from a short list and the choice is inevitably subjective. However, here are twenty books that the authors have found personally useful for evangelism and apologetics in the European context. We suggest that those trying to reach Europeans today should be familiar with at least a representative selection of these titles.

Richard Bauckham, *Jesus and the Eyewitnesses: The Gospels as Eyewitness Testimony*, Grand Rapids MI: Eerdmans, 2017

William Lane Craig, *Reasonable Faith: Christian Truth and Apologetics*, Wheaton IL: Crossway Books, third ed., 2008

Paul Copan, *Is God a Moral Monster? Making Sense of the Old Testament God*, Grand Rapids MI: Baker, 2011

Sharon Dirckx, *Why? Looking at God, Evil and Personal Suffering*, London: IVP, 2013

Amy Orr-Ewing, *Where is God in all the Suffering?*, Epsom, Surrey: The Good Book Company, 2020

Norman L. Geisler, *The Big Book of Christian Apologetics: An A to Z Guide*, Grand Rapids MI: Baker, 2012

Douglas Groothuis, *Christian Apologetics: A Comprehensive Case for Christian Faith*, London: IVP, second ed., 2022

Gary Habermas & Mike Licona, *The Case for the Resurrection of Jesus*, Grand Rapids MI: Kregel, 2004

Timothy Keller, *The Reason for God: Belief in an Age of Scepticism,* London: Hodder & Stoughton, 2008

John Lennox, *Can Science Explain Everything?,* Epsom, Surrey: The Good Book Company, 2019

John Lennox, *Cosmic Chemistry: Do God and Science Mix?,* London: Lion, 2021

Stephen C. Meyer, *Signature in the Cell: DNA and the Evidence for Intelligent Design,* New York NY: Harper One, 2009

Josh McDowell & Sean McDowell, *Evidence for Jesus: Timeless Answers to Tough Questions,* Grand Rapids MI: Zondervan, 2023

Rebecca McLaughlin, *Confronting Christianity:12 Hard Questions for the World's Largest Religion,* Wheaton IL: Crossway Books, 2019

Beth Peltola & Tim Dieppe, *Questions to Ask Your Muslim Friends: A Closer Look at Islamic Beliefs and Texts,* London: Wilberforce Publications, 2022

Beth Peltola, *A Short Guide to Islam: A Biblical Response to the Faith of our Muslim Neighbours,* Brentwood TN: B & H Publishing, 2023

Lee Strobel, *The Case for Christ: A Journalist's Personal Investigation of the Evidence for Jesus,* Grand Rapids MI: Zondervan, 1998

Gene Edward Veith, Jr., *Post-Christian: A Guide to Contemporary Thought and Culture,* Wheaton IL: Crossway, 2020

Peter Williams, *Can we Trust the Gospels?,* Wheaton IL: Crossway, 2018

N. T. Wright, *Simply Jesus: Who he was, what he did, why it matters,* London: SPCK, 2011

Key statistics on Europe

GREATER EUROPE
Demographic, Economic, and Religious Dimensions

	Population	Population change	Natural pop. inc. rate (number/ 1000 pop) (2022)	Population density (persons/ sq.km)	GDP ($US billion)	GDP/ head ($US)
Scandinavian North						
Denmark	5,932,654	↑	1.7	130	406	67,218
Faroes	54,255	↔	6.3	36	3	51,995
Finland	5,538,238	↑	0	17	302	56,391
Sweden	10,521,556	↑	1.3	22	624	58,997
Iceland	390,830	↑	6.4	3	29	72,231
Greenland	56,446	↔	4.8	0.03	N/A	57,116
Norway	5,434,319	↑	4.0	14	554	81,995
Total	*27,928,298*				*1,918*	*64,869*
The Mid West						
UK	67,026,292	↑	1.7	280	3,159	46,344
Ireland	5,123,536	↑	5.6	70	594	94,556
Germany	84,270,625	↓	-2.9	230	4,309	53,988
Czechia	10,526,937	↔	-2.1	130	330	25,732
Austria	9,106,126	↑	-0.4	100	515	53,859
Switzerland	8,740,472	↑	2.0	210	870	94,696
France	68,042,591	↑	2.2	120	2,923	44,995
Belgium	11,665,930	↑	1.4	380	554	50,103
The Netherlands	17,858,790	↑	1.8	410	1,081	61,516
Luxembourg	647,599	↑	4.4	230	87	138,772
Liechtenstein	39,327	↑	2.3	240	N/A	
Monaco	36.469	↑	-4.3	19600	N/A	
Total	*283,048,261*				*14,422*	*64,144*
The Sunshine States						
Spain	47,558,630	↔	-3.1	92	1,398	30,996
Portugal	10,270,865	↓	-2.9	110	268	25,065
Gibraltar (UK)	32,649	↔	5.1	5,800	0.599	18,352
Italy	58,883,079	↓	-4.3	200	2,170	34,997
Malta	533,286	↑	1.2	1,400	19	31,576
Andorra	79,824	↓	-1.0	160	4	50,110
San Marino	33,661	↑		550	2	51,753

---

1. Different statisticians use different methodologies for counting evangelicals in a given population. The data in this table and the following table are taken from the *World Christian Encyclopedia* and they differ somewhat from the data given elsewhere in this volume from *Operation World*. For the purposes of this volume, we have assumed that evangelicals, Pentecostals and Charismatics should all be regarded as Christians in the biblical sense.

2. Figure from UK Census, 2021.

Total Christian (%)	Catholic (%)	Protestant (%)	Ind. & Unaffiliated (%)	Orthodox (%)	Evangelical, Pentecostal & Charismatic (%)[1]	Muslim (%)	Non-religious (%)
80	1	76	3	1	6	5	14
98		96	2		28		2
77		71	5	1	15	3	19
59	1	57	1	1	9	9	32
92	4	79	10	1	7		6
96		63	32		16		3
85	3	82	11		10	7	8
[46][2]	10	40	17	1	14	7	[37][2]
93	75	3.5	13		12	2	7
66	29	30	5	3	3	7	27
35	31	4	2		3		64
71	61	4	5	2	7	7	21
74	40	29	4	2	7	3	19
63	57	1	4	1	2	9	25
63	60	1	1	1	3	8	28
55	26	16	13		6	7	35
77	74	2	2		4	3	20
88	71	10	7	1	3	1	5
85	82	3	1		3		13
87	84	3	2	2	3	3	11
89	85	1	4		7	1	9
89	80	7	2		10	5	2
76	73	1	2	2	2	6	17
96	90		1	1	10	2	2
90	85		6		1	2	7
92	85		6		2		8

	Population	Population change	Natural pop. inc. rate (number/ 1000 pop) (2022)	Population density (persons/ sq.km)	GDP ($US billion)	GDP/ head ($US)
Vatican City	519	↔				21,198
Total	*117,392,513*				*3,862*	*32,506*
Central & Eastern Europe						
Poland	37,749,000	↓	-2.2	120	599	18,109
Hungary	9,678,000	↓	-4.2	100	188	18,075
Slovakia	5,428,792	↔	-1.2	110	127	21,529
Romania	19,053,815	↓	-6.5	82	349	14,968
Lithuania	2,750,055	↓	-5.8	44	78	22,245
Latvia	1,850,651	↓	-6	29	47	19,824
Estonia	1,326,062	↓	-4.3	29	41	26,470
Moldova	3,272,996	↓	-2.3	120	16	3,096
Belarus	9,534,955	↓	-3.8	45	73	10,487
Ukraine	39,701,739	↓	-4.8	72	149	3,753
Total	*90,644,326*				*1518*	*12,659*
The Balkans						
Greece	10,432,481	↓	-4.4	84	239	19,673
Slovenia	2,119,844	↓	-2.1	100	68	32,078
Croatia	3,871,833	↓	-4.2	73	79	16,247
Serbia	6,647,003	↓		85	74	8,748
Bosnia-Herzegovina	3,320,954	↓	-1.9	68	28	7,041
Montenegro	617,683	↔	0.9	46	7	9,545
Kosovo	1,659,714	↑	6.8	190	10	4,401
Albania	2,793,592	↔	5.4	100	20	6,285
North Macedonia	1,832,696	↔	0.9	81	15	6,657
Bulgaria	6,781,953	↓		63	101	11,321
Total	*40,077,753*				*641*	*13,409*
The Levant						
Turkey	85,816,199	↑	8.2	110	1,029	9,407
Cyprus (inc. North Cyprus)	1,251,489	↑	3.7	130	31	29,551
Israel[3]	9,038,309	↑	12.3	430	564	62,401
Lebanon	5,489,740	↑	7.5	590	19	2,500
Total	*101,595,737*				*1,643*	*36,744*

Source: *World Christian Encyclopedia Online*, Todd M. Johnson, Gina A. Zurlo. Consulted online on 05 March 2024 <http://dx.doi.org/10.1163/2666-6855_WCEO_COM_02ALB>
First published online: 2020
Percentages for religious populations are estimates for 2020.

---

3. In addition to the religious percentages given against Israel in this table, 71% of the population of Israel are Jewish by religion.

Total Christian (%)	Catholic (%)	Protestant (%)	Ind. & Unaffiliated (%)	Orthodox (%)	Evangelical, Pentecostal & Charismatic (%)	Muslim (%)	Non-religious (%)
96	90		5	2	5		4
87	60	26	2	2	8		12
85	73	8	4	1	6	1	15
99	7	10	1	88	13	1	1
89	77	2	6	5	2		11
82	23	37	1	23	18		17
37		15	10	12	8		63
98	1	1	1	95	2		2
79	11	3	5	60	3		21
86	11	2	2	73	4	2	12
89	1		1	87	1	6	5
82	74	2	4	3	3	4	14
94	84	1	4	6	3	2	4
90	6	1	5	84	2	7	3
49	12			38	1	48	3
79	4	3	2	71	6	17	3
6	3	1		3	0.4	93	1
37	18		1	18	2	60	2.5
64	1	1		63	1	33	3
83	1	2	1	81	4	14	3
						98	1
70	1	1	2	66	2	23	5
2	1			1	1		6
35	28	1	1	6	1	59	4

GREATER EUROPE
Evolution of Religious Practice and Commitment 1900-2020
All figures are % of total population

	1900					1970				
	Catholic	Ortho-dox	Prot	Ev/Ch/Pent	Non-rel.	Catholic	Ortho-dox	Prot	Ev/Ch/Pent	Non-rel.
Scandinavian North										
Denmark			99	15	0.2	1		96	6	3
Faroes			100	50	0			100	21	0
Finland			97	21	0			94	12	3.5
Sweden			99	59	1			75	18	25
Iceland			99.5	30	0.1			96	3	1
Greenland			80	44	0			76	4	0.2
Norway			99	61	1			99	12	1
Total										
The Mid West										
UK	6		88	50	2	10		66	27	8
Ireland	89		10	8	0	91		4	4	0.4
Germany	36		61	9	0.3	36		44	3	10
Czechia	86		6	1	9.4	59		4	2	19
Austria	92		3	0.3	0.2	88		6	1	3
Switzerland	40		56	14	0.2	46		46	6	1
France	98		2	0.3	0.3	82		2	1	12
Belgium	97		0.4	0.1	1	90		1	0.4	6
The Netherlands	97		1	1	0	87		2	0.3	4
Luxembourg										
Liechtenstein										
Monaco										
Total										
The Sunshine States										
Spain	100		0	0	0	97		0.2	0.3	2
Portugal	100		0	0	0	92		1	1	4
Gibraltar (UK)										
Italy	100		0.2	0.1	0.2	88		1	1	11
Malta	88		5	0.3	0	9.3		1	0.1	0.5
Andorra										
San Marino										
Vatican City										
Total										

	2000					2020			
Catholic	Ortho-dox	Prot	Ev/Ch/ Pent	Non-rel.	Catholic	Ortho-dox	Prot	Ev/Ch/ Pent	Non-rel.
1		86	6	9	1		76	6	14
0.3		96	26	1.6	0.4		96	28	1.8
		76	16	17			71	15	20
1		64	11	29	1		56	9	32
2		94	9	3	4		79	8	6
0.2		68	14	2	0.2		64	16	3
1		90	12	5	3		72	10	8
10		50	15	19	10		40	15	23
82		4	15	3	75		4	12	7
33		34	3	21	29		31	3	26
36		2	3	60	31		2	3	64
73		5	4	12	61		4	4	21
43		35	8	11	39		30	7	19
62		2	3	21	57		1	2	25
72		1	3	20	60		1	3	28
87		2	4	9	75		2	4	20
89		0.2	3	8	84		0.3	4	11
89		1	6	6	85		1	7	9
79		1	3	16	73		1	3	17
92		0.4	10	2	90		0.3	10	2

	1900					1970				
	Catholic	Ortho-dox	Prot	Ev/Ch/Pent	Non-rel.	Catholic	Ortho-dox	Prot	Ev/Ch/Pent	Non-rel.
Central & Eastern Europe										
Poland	77		3	0.5	0.1	88		0.5	0.1	10
Hungary	61		27	3	0.5	59		24	5	14
Slovakia	73		19	1	0.2	78		18	4	14
Romania	1	88	1.3	1	0.3	14	79	8	5	15
Lithuania	90	3	0.5	0.5	0.1	66	4	1	0.3	29
Latvia	33	15	45	20	0.1	14	11	16	5	60
Estonia	1	43	54	30	0.2	0.2	21	24	8	54
Moldova	2	89	1	1	0.2	2	43	1	0.5	52
Belarus	30	56	0.1	0.1	0.4	9	49	0.2	0.3	40
Ukraine	18	71	2	2	0.2	4	54	3	2	38
Total										
The Balkans										
Greece	2	84	0.2	0.1	0	0.5	97	0.3	0.2	0.2
Slovenia	95	0.1	0.1	0.1	0	88	2	2	0.4	7
Croatia	82	10	0.1	0.1	4	82	8	1	0.4	3
Serbia	10	77	5	1	0.2	8	54	2	1	31
Bosnia-Herzegovina	17	43	0	0	0	17	27	0	0	18
Montenegro	6	88	0	0	0	6	43	1	1	37
Kosovo	3	9	0.1	0	1	3	7	0.1	0.1	5
Albania	8	20	0	0	0.1	3	5	0	0	63
North Macedonia	1	63	0.1	0.1	0	2.3	66	0.1	0	8
Bulgaria	1	76	0.1	0.1	0.1	1	65	1	1	22
Total										
The Levant										
Turkey										
Cyprus (inc. North Cyprus)	1	77	0.1	0	0	1	73	2	1	2
Israel										
Lebanon										

Source: *World Christian Encyclopedia Online* (Brill)

		2000					2020		
Catholic	Ortho-dox	Prot	Ev/Ch/Pent	Non-rel.	Catholic	Ortho-dox	Prot	Ev/Ch/Pent	Non-rel.
92		0.3	0.1	4	90		0.4	0.3	4
61		23	9	12	60		26	8	12
68		10	6	16	73		8	6	15
10	87	8	10	1	7	88	9	13	1
77	5	1	2	12.4	77	5	1.5	2	11
17	17	23	10	43	23	23	37	18	17
0.3	11	16	8	61	0.4	12	15	8	63
1	93	2	2	3.4	1	95	1	2	2
11	53	1	2	30	11	60	3	3	21
9	69	2	3	18	11	71	2	4	12
0.5	92	0.2	1	2.6	1	87	0.2	1	5
82	3	1	2	8	74	3	2	3	14
81	6	1	5	7	84	6	1	3	4
5	85	1	2	5	6	84	1	2	3
12	37	0.1	1	5	12	38	0.2	1	3
4	65	2	4	11	4	79	3	6	3
3	3	0.1	0.3	1	3	3	1	0.4	1
15	12	0.2	1	7	18	18	1	2	3
1	62	0.4	1	5	1	63	0.4	1	3
1	82	2	3	4	1	81	2	4	3
1	66	2	2	4	1	66	1	2	5

An outline of European institutions[1]

Over the past 200 years, the role and character of the nation state has become more clearly defined than previously, as discussed in chapter 2 above. One result is that all human beings are expected to be citizens of some nation state or other (and a relatively few can have dual or multiple nationalities); and it is serious matter for any individual to become stateless. At the same time, in a globalizing world it is essential for nation states to cooperate at least on some matters, and, to do that effectively, they need to commit themselves collectively to international arrangements governing the matters in view. Such international arrangements relate not just to trade, defence, and migration, but to a host of less-noticed matters like sea and air navigation, road transport signage in a place like Europe, environmental matters which often need trans-boundary regulation and sometimes global regulation, and health (since bacilli and viruses do not recognize international boundaries and people travel a lot).

These international arrangements are normally established under treaties between the states concerned. These treaties form part of the body of international law. They can be bilateral or multilateral. Normally, they require the agreement of all parties in order to be effective both initially and when altered, and individual parties each therefore have a veto: it is rarer for a majority of parties to be able to impose arrangements with which a party or parties disagree.[2] Very often treaties provide for arbitration in the event that

---

1. This appendix depends to a considerable extent for factual information on the relevant entries in Wikipedia. In recognition of this, a donation has been made to Wikipedia.

2. An important, rare example of such majority control is the European Union which, from early on, put the larger countries in a position collectively to control decisions in the Council of Ministers—while the Maastricht Treaty of 1992 significantly extended the policy areas subject

one party has a grievance against its counter-party which arises under the particular treaty. Multilateral treaties, depending on their nature, may establish a court to adjudicate matters under the treaty (for example, the World Trade Organization has an Appellate Body, a court of appeal, which sits in Geneva).

The number and complexity of these treaties grew rapidly in the twentieth century, though apparently the oldest multilateral organization still in operation was established by the Congress of Vienna in 1815. That is the Central Commission for Navigation on the Rhine,[3] whose basic navigation rules have been in force since 1831. The navigability of the Rhine was key to economic development in the basin in the 1800s and it remains an important artery for inland shipping. But of more prominence now are the Commissions on the Protection of the Rhine and Danube respectively, which enable joint international action on flooding, water resources and water quality.

The scale and variety of such international cooperation in Europe is understandably confusing for anyone who does not take a close interest in such matters. The remainder of this appendix summarizes the key international arrangements in Europe. The outline is intended as background briefing for those who are involved in mission to Europe or who are considering it, as it helps them to know how Europe works.

The European Union

The European Union (EU) derives from concerns in the immediate aftermath of World War 2 that greater European integration would (1) contain difficulty and war arising from the presence in Europe of a number of powerful nation states; (2) revive the war-depleted European economy; and (3) resist further westward encroachment by the Soviet Union and its client states in eastern Europe. Initial steps included a coal and steel community, and cooperation with respect to atomic energy. In 1957, the first six member states agreed to establish the European Economic Community and the European Atomic Energy Community.

---

to qualified majority voting in the Council and also brought the directly-elected European Parliament into the decision-making process under co-decision procedures.

3. The UK was a member between 1919 and 1993, because of its interest in Rhine navigation.

The main immediate instrument of the EEC was a customs union, on the lines of the customs union which had facilitated German unification in the nineteenth century. The customs union was eventually underpinned in the 1980s by the establishment of a single market in many goods. Since then, there has been a number of important developments in the direction of enhanced integration, and also aspirations to give the EU institutions a role in foreign policy and possibly in defence, separate from those of the member states. There have also been constitutional developments which have enhanced the role of the European Parliament in enacting legislation, so that decision-making in the Union is now in part a matter of agreement between the member states and in part at the will of the directly-elected European Parliament (in practice, there needs to be negotiation between the two in order to arrive at agreed legislation). Also, on some legislative matters and decisions within the competence of the Union, individual member states no longer have a veto; decisions on those matters can be taken by qualified majority of the member states (which encourages alliance-building between member states, rather than seeking the consensus of all which is necessary when all have a veto—a consensus which often may have the characteristics of a lowest common denominator).

Efforts at creating a single currency for the Union (the Eurozone) and borderless movement of people between member states (the Schengen area) have been only partially successful: 12 of the present 27 member states are members of the Eurozone, while 23 out of 27 member states, plus the members of the European Free Trade Association (Iceland, Leichtenstein, Norway and Switzerland) permit movement between themselves without border checks (Bulgaria, Cyprus and Romania retain border checks, and Ireland is not a party to the Schengen agreement, preferring to retain membership of the Common Travel Area with the UK). In foreign affairs, the Union is now separately represented in many forums, alongside the representatives of member states. Little progress has been made so far in enhancing the Union's role in defence matters (which is complicated by the existence of the North Atlantic Treaty Organisation (NATO) as the main organisation for the defence of Europe).

In addition to the present 27 member states of the EU, there are currently nine recognized candidates for membership of the EU (Albania, Bosnia and Herzegovina, Georgia, Moldova, Montenegro, North Macedonia, Serbia, and

Turkey) and one that is recognized to be a potential candidate (Kosovo). Recognition of Ukraine as a candidate is under discussion. Candidate states negotiate terms of accession, which are often of a transitional character, and must align their domestic law with the body of EU law before joining.

The EU has three key constitutional institutions: (1) the European Commission (in effect, the government departments of the Union); the Commission alone has the power to propose new legislation to the Council and Parliament, though the Parliament can ask the Commission to prepare legislation; (2) the European Council which is the representatives of the member states meeting formally to consider matters of Union business (there are Council meetings, i.e., of the relevant ministers of member states, for each area of EU competence, e.g., an Environment Council, a Finance Council, an Agriculture Council, and so on); and (3) the European Parliament which has been directly elected every four years since 1979.

The questions of whether or not the EU has competence to legislate in particular matters, and whether that competence is exclusive to it or is shared with member states, are important. In summary, the position is as follows:

Exclusive competence on the part of the EU

- customs union
- competition rules for the single market
- monetary policy for the eurozone countries
- trade and international agreements (under certain circumstances)
- marine plants and animals regulated by the common fisheries policy

Competence shared between EU and member states

- single market
- employment and social affairs
- economic, social and territorial cohesion
- agriculture
- fisheries
- environment
- consumer protection
- transport
- trans-European networks

- energy
- justice and fundamental rights
- migration and home affairs
- public health (for the aspects defined in Article 168 of the Treaty on the Functioning of the European Union)
- research and space
- development cooperation and humanitarian aid

Matters where there is no EU competence and its role is no more than to support member states in the administration of the matters concerned

- public health
- industry
- culture
- tourism
- education and training, youth and sport
- civil protection
- administrative cooperation

The treaties set out three principles on which it is to be determined how and in what matters the EU may act:

- conferral—the EU has only that authority conferred upon it by the EU treaties
- proportionality—EU action cannot exceed what is necessary to achieve the objectives of the treaties
- subsidiarity—in areas where either the EU or national governments can act, the EU may intervene only if it can act more effectively than national governments.

In practice in relation to any relevant matter, the last two principles leave scope for discussion, debate and dispute as to the role of the EU.

The Court of Justice of the European Union (ECJ) acts as an administrative court and a constitutional court for the European Union. It can annul legislative acts of the EU (e.g., regulations and directives), and acts of its institutions, including the Council, the Commission, the European

Central Bank, and EU offices and agencies, often but not always in respect of action affecting third parties. It also enforces EU law, including where member states are alleged by the European Commission to have failed to implement directives correctly either as to their intent or in practice. Enforcement action can include fining member states for lack of action or defective action. It is this last area of action by the Court which has led to criticism of the Court itself in member states, including for infringing the sovereignty of individual member states (though usually the Court is doing no more than to adjudicate matters in which sovereignty was ceded in the act of joining the EU). It should be noted that the ECJ would only be involved in adjudicating matters relating to migration when they arise from the EU's own actions in respect of migration or its member states' implementation of such actions. But concerns about the role of a European Court with respect to migration are, mainly, not properly directed at the ECJ, but to the European Court of Human Rights, a quite separate body operating under different collective arrangements agreed by European nation states (see below).

There is also a EU Court of Auditors, the purpose of which is to audit the financial activities of the EU, its institutions and bodies, offices and agencies. It has not been reluctant to expose malpractice and poor value for money, when necessary.

The European Economic Area (EEA) and the European Free Trade Association (EFTA)

The EEA came into being at the beginning of 1994 following an agreement between the EU and its member states with the states of EFTA. By the time of the agreement, the EFTA states were reduced to four, as a result of successful application by other EFTA states (Sweden, Finland and Austria) to become member states of the EU. Switzerland had the opportunity to join the EEA, but its people rejected the proposal on referendum.[4] Thus the EEA comprises the 27 EU states and Iceland, Norway and Liechtenstein. The agreement extends the EU single market to the three non-EU states, allowing free movement of persons, goods, services, and capital in the extended market. Citizens of the

4. As a result, Switzerland also suspended its application to join the EU and instead negotiated bilateral trade agreements with the EU.

30 member states can reside in any of them as they wish. The agreement is focussed on strengthening trade and economic relations, but the Common Agricultural Policy and the Common Fisheries Policy of the EU do not extend to the three additional states. The three states are also outside the EU Customs Union and are therefore subject to any border tariffs which the EU may maintain for the Customs Union.

The Council of Europe (CE)

The Council of Europe is a completely distinct organisation from the EU. Chronologically, it was the first effort to give effect to the desire for European integration after World War 2.[5] The proposal for such an organisation was first made in March 1943 by Winston Churchill in a wartime broadcast. The CE was formed in 1949, but some looking for it to develop into a united states of Europe soon became disillusioned and shifted their hopes to the bodies which preceded creation of the European Economic Community in 1957, the forerunner of the EU (see above).

In 2023, the CE comprises 46 member states and includes all states on the European landmass apart from Belarus and Russia (the latter was excluded from the organisation at the end of 2022, following the invasion of Ukraine (a member)). In addition, Iceland, Turkey, Armenia, Azerbaijan and Georgia are members. The organisation is governed by a Committee of Ministers (the foreign ministers of the member states) and a Parliamentary Assembly comprising parliamentarians nominated by each member state (reflecting the party distribution in the parliament of the particular nominating state). Membership is open to any European state provided that it 'accept[s] the principles of the rule of law and the enjoyment by all persons within its jurisdiction of human rights and fundamental freedoms' and is willing to 'collaborate sincerely and effectively' in the work of the Council.

The CE's sphere of activities is protecting the rule of law and fostering legal cooperation between states; coordination of counter-terrorism measures; the efficiency of justice; protection of human rights across their full range (including prevention of torture, countering racism and intolerance, countering

---

5. Or perhaps the second, given that the UNECE, was established in 1947, with somewhat similar objectives (see below).

human trafficking, protecting personal data, preventing and combating sexual exploitation, sexual abuse, and violence against women, and protecting and promoting social rights, local government, linguistic and minority rights, and press freedom). It also protects democracy through election monitoring and democratic reforms, promotes cultural cooperation, the right to education, fair sport, youth exchanges, and the quality of medicine. Some of this is done through a range of semi-autonomous bodies with which the CE has agreements (for example, the European Directorate for the Quality of Medicines, the Cooperation Group to Combat Drug Abuse and Illicit Trafficking in Drugs, and the Group of States Against Corruption).

A key early achievement of the CE was the **European Convention on Human Rights** [and Fundamental Freedoms] agreed in 1950. That Convention provided for the establishment of the **European Court of Human Rights** (located in Strasbourg, along with the administrative headquarters of the CE). This comprises a judge from each member state, elected for a non-renewable term of nine years by the Parliamentary Assembly of the CE. It is this court (not any EU institution), to which appeal may be made from member states on matters of human rights under the European Convention on Human Rights. (It is this body which some in the UK fear may interfere in the UK's ability to transfer asylum seekers for processing in Rwanda.)

It is apparent that the CE is a body which is committed to protecting and promoting the rule of law, democracy, human rights, fundamental freedoms, and combating a variety of abuses, including drug and people trafficking, sexual abuse, corruption, and restrictions on press freedom (even if the records of some of its member states are not entirely unblemished on some of these matters!). In becoming a member state of the CE, the member state concerned cedes sovereignty to the CE in these particulars. Withdrawing from the Convention would presumably raise the question whether the member state should be suspended, or even excluded, from the CE.

NATO

The North Atlantic Treaty establishing NATO was signed on 4 April 1949. There were 12 founding members (the USA and Canada and 10 European states). With expansion in eastern Europe after the collapse of the Warsaw

Pact, there will be 32 members once the accession process for Sweden is completed. There are three current candidates for membership: Bosnia and Herzegovina, Georgia and Ukraine. As is typical in many such international arrangements (including, for example, the United Nations), collective decision-making depends on the assent of all the parties to the Treaty. Depending on the circumstances, at key moments, this can give significant influence to individual members to pursue a matter that they perceive to be in their national interest. It is for this reason that Turkey and Hungary were able to delay the accession of Sweden to the Treaty, in the case of Turkey, arising out of a dispute between Turkey and Sweden about Kurdish citizens of Turkey (Turkey would say, terrorists) who have sought asylum in Sweden.

The military alliance was formed in response to the new situation in Europe following 1945, when it became clear that the Soviet Union intended to control the countries of eastern Europe behind the final line of the Soviet armies' advance into Europe in 1945 and to see Communist governments installed elsewhere in Europe if possible. The alliance was to provide collective security to its members on the principle outlined in article 5 of the Treaty: that each member state is to consider an armed attack against one member state, in territories in Europe, North America, Turkey, and Atlantic islands north of the Tropic of Cancer, to be an armed attack against them all. In such a case, each member state is required to take such action as that member state deems necessary, including the use of armed force, to restore and maintain the security of the North Atlantic area: in brief, an attack on one is to be deemed an attack on all, to which all must respond appropriately.

Article 5 has been invoked only once, following the terrorist attack on the Twin Towers in New York on 11 September 2001. This led to NATO action in a number of places, including Afghanistan over an extended period ending in 2021, and Iraq in 2003 and subsequently. In the 1990s, NATO took joint military action in Yugoslavia, first, in the Bosnian war of 1992–95, mainly through aerial bombardment, at the request of the United Nations, to assist in enforcing Security Council resolutions aimed at restraining Serbian military action in Bosnia;[6] and, secondly, in the Kosovo war in 1999, without

---

6. NATO members with reservations did not exercise their veto.

UN agreement but on the grounds of humanitarian intervention (a provision under international law which permits cross-border use of military force in extreme circumstances to end severe and widespread violations of human rights). With the support of NATO, member states have been giving military assistance to Ukraine following the Russian invasions of 2014 and 2021. Otherwise, the main military function of NATO was the deterrence of the Soviet Union during the Cold War (1949–91). For most of its existence, crucial to the effectiveness of NATO has been the military contribution (and expenditure) of the USA to the alliance. In recent years, there has been some recognition on the part of European member states of the need to contribute more, proportionally, to the military effectiveness of the alliance.

Other international organisations in or of relevance to Europe

The focus of this appendix has been on the major international arrangements for collective action between states in Europe. From references already made, it will be clear that there is a wide range of multilateral and bilateral agreements which have been made by European states between themselves in order collectively to obtain mutual advantage of one sort or another. Three other multilateral arrangements of wide scope can be mentioned here.

First, the **United Nations Economic Commission for Europe (UNECE).** Within the United Nations, member states are grouped into regional organisations in each part of the world. That for Europe is described as the Economic Commission for Europe. Established in 1947, the purpose was to facilitate concerted action for the economic reconstruction of Europe and to strengthen the economic relations of European countries between themselves and with other countries. UNECE has 56 member states, which, in addition to obviously European states, include the USA and Canada, Russia, the states in the Caucasus area, and the Stans, that is stretching eastwards from the Pacific coast of north America as far as the borders of China.

Between 1947 and 1991, the work of UNECE was hampered by the division of Europe between western and eastern blocs, and since 1991 it has in effect been subordinate to, in particular, the extension of the EU eastwards. In relation to its underlying objectives, the UNECE quickly found itself either stymied by the divisions of Europe or superseded by competing international structures. Now much of its work is in the area of monitoring and statistics in relation to the subjects which it covers. But it has a significant role in inland transport, in particular by providing the secretariat of the World Forum on Harmonization of Vehicle Regulations (which obviously facilitates, through global UN agreements, the production of vehicles which are saleable and operable anywhere in the world) and the TIR system which facilitates the transit of customs posts by international freight transport.

Second, there is the **Organisation for Economic Cooperation and Development (OECD).** Its origins lie in the Organisation for European Economic Cooperation, established in 1948 to help to administer the Marshall Plan of US aid for the economic reconstruction of Europe following World War 2. As such, it was a body confined to western Europe (it had a sort of counterpart in the eastern bloc, though that worked on different economic principles). It was reformed in 1961 as the OECD, over time including the main non-European free-market states. The member states are committed to democracy and market economies, and the underlying purpose is to stimulate growth and world trade. There are 38 member states, skewed towards those with high income and development. It has significant global roles in relation to tax and statistical matters, and definitions for the purpose of meaningful international statistical comparisons.

Third, there is the **Organization for Security and Cooperation in Europe (OSCE).** It is not an international body established by treaty between the member states, but results from a political commitment by the heads of government of the signatories. It does not have legal personality and its charter does not have the status of international law. Political direction is by rare summits of heads of states. A ministerial council meets annually, and a permanent council of ambassadors of member states meets weekly. A Forum for Security Cooperation decides on matters of military cooperation. The OSCE has a Parliamentary Assembly of parliamentarians of the member states. There are 57 member states, embracing North America, Europe, Turkey and the territories of the former Soviet Union.

The OSCE's origins are in the early 1970s when the need was perceived for a forum in which the western and eastern blocs could discuss security matters in order to try to improve relations between east and west at a time of great and permanent military risk. Its focus now is on arms control, the promotion of human rights, freedom of the press, and fair and free elections. To that extent, there is some considerable overlap with the ambit of the CE, though it unlikely that the expansion of the CE would have been acceptable to the eastern bloc in the early 1970s. Practically and on the ground, the OSCE operates by sending missions to areas of tension with a view to seeking political solutions which avoid or conclude conflict and promote the protection of human rights; and in providing missions to monitor whether elections can be regarded as free and fair (this has included monitoring elections at state level in the USA).

Bearing in mind that this account of multilateral bodies established for collective action by the nation states of Europe focuses only a very few of the most important of them, it is difficult to escape the conclusion that the pattern is complex and something of a patchwork. If the origins of each body are considered, the significance of immediate events and urgency comes to mind. Human beings cannot see the future or at least only very dimly. The decision-makers also have limited knowledge of existing bodies and their remits, though it is to be hoped that officials are not so ill-informed (though they too often work in silos, so that they know of the bodies within their areas of responsibility, but not necessarily of those in somebody else's purview). Decision-makers also have personal, public and political reasons for being seen to have created a new body rather than adapting one created by predecessors. And the sharp division of Europe into two armed camps between 1947 and 1991 constrained what was possible: UNECE and OSCE excepted, it is only since 1991 that some of the bodies referred to above have been able to enlarge themselves to cover Europe as a whole. Nevertheless, if the system were being created from scratch, it is not apparent that the result would be anything like the pattern that we have now.

Illustrations acknowledgements

These notes indicate the basis on which illustrations have been reprinted in this volume.

The Emperor Constantine (p. 4): Alamy—licence purchased.

Francis Bacon (p. 8): Photographic reproduction of public domain artwork ({{PD-Art}}). Portrait by Paul van Somer I, 1617 (Łazienki Palace, Warsaw).

Galileo Galilei (p. 8): Photographic reproduction of public domain artwork ({{PD-art}}). Portrait by Justus Sustermans (National Maritime Museum, Greenwich).

Isaac Newton (p. 9): Photographic reproduction of public domain artwork ({{PD-Art}}). Portrait by Godfrey Kneller, 1689.

René Descartes (p.11): Photographic reproduction of public domain artwork ({{PD-Art}}). Portrait after Franz Hals (Louvre Museum, Paris).

Friedrich Nietzsche (p. 13): Photograph in the public domain. By Friedrich Hermann Hartmann, c. 1875.

Hereford Mappa Mundi (p 20): Photographic reproduction of public domain item ({{PD-art}}), c. 1300, displayed in Hereford Cathedral, England.

Hitler (p. 23): licensed under the Creative Commons Attribution-Share Alike 3.0 Germany license.

NATO (p. 25): Photograph in the public domain (work of the US federal government).